# Praise for *Glow In* ~~T~~

'*Glow In The Dark* is a transformative guide to becoming and broadcasting – your authentic self in order to connect with your audience, build your business, and actually enjoy the process. With wit, warmth, and the benefit of his own considerable experience and success, Mark will convince you why your personal story is important, and show you how to tell it. He is a gem, and this book is gold.'

Sarah Knight, *New York Times* bestselling author of the *No F\*\*ks Given Guides*

'Personal storytelling is a powerful way to build a truly meaningful connection with others. In *Glow In The Dark*, Mark Leruste provides a brilliant and compassionate guide to connecting with your authentic self and finding the courage to share your personal story in a way that will inspire others into action. His advice is practical and compelling. A must-read for entrepreneurs and business leaders.'

Scott Harrison, Founder and CEO, charity: water

'Finally a book that not only talks about the value of sharing our personal story to better connect and engage with our audience but actually shows you how to do it in a simple and practical way.'

Nir Eyal, *Wall Street Journal* bestselling author of *Hooked* and *Indistractable*

'If you want to stand out from the crowd and be remembered you need to read this book. Simple, powerful, actionable.'

Shaa Wasmund, bestselling author of
*Stop Talking, Start Doing*

'A must read for every entrepreneur and business leader who wants to raise their profile and turn their personal story into a powerful asset that gets noticed.'

Daniel Priestley, Co-Founder and CEO of
Dent Global and bestselling author of
*Key Person of Influence*

'Mark's book shows us how powerful our stories can be when we develop the courage to share them. His practical tips help us unearth the connective stories each of us has – and Mark shows us that when we tell them, they can create impact beyond what we imagined.'

Emily Gindlesparger, author of
*Please Make Me Love Me*

'Our species survived and thrived because of our ability to tell a good story. Today we need the positive stories of the people and ideas solving the world's biggest problems to spread far and fast. Mark is the ideal guide to help our stories glow bright in dark times.'

Ben Keene, Co-Founder of
Rebel Book Club and Raaise

'I feel like Mark Leruste has written this book from inside my head. I love the work I do, but I hate having to create content and put myself out there. This book is human, funny and intensely practical. It is already helping me remove some of the 'ickiness' from the idea of telling my story. Thank you, Mark!'

Graham Allcott, Founder of Think Productive and bestselling author of *How to be a Productivity Ninja*

'As entrepreneurs, the road we travel is often neither straightforward or paved with gold. But all the bumps and bruises we get along the way are what make us perfectly placed to help others on their road to success. I learnt this when I worked with Mark to share my story authentically with the world. Mark is the perfect guide to support you on your journey of personal discovery and professional freedom, and his incredible knowledge, insights and compassion that he shares so generously in his book will help you tell your story in a way you never believed possible.'

Donna O'Toole, Founder and CEO of August Recognition and author of *Win!*

'*Glow In The Dark* is a remarkable book that effectively conveys how sharing your story authentically can yield unprecedented results. Do me a favour, if you have something important to say or share and want to make a positive impact with your work, don't waste another minute, read Mark's book.'

Dr Rupy Aujla, bestselling author and Founder of *The Doctor's Kitchen*

'Mark taught me that sharing your story is the most powerful way to create a sacred sense of connection between you and your audience. I feel it's the reason why I've been invited on so many platforms to share my story. So if you feel you have a message to share with the world, then this book is going to be a great gift for you and those who are waiting to hear form you. I can't wait for you to read it.'

Tony Riddle, Founder of The Natural Life-Stylist and bestselling author of *Be More Human*

'An inspiring book for impact-driven leaders that will change how you approach storytelling. Mark Leruste gives you the courage to stop feeling like an imposter and share your story authentically.'

Jadah Sellner, bestselling author of *Simple Green Smoothies* and *She Builds* and host of Lead with Love podcast

'It's easy to get story envy when you listen to someone else. Then you fall into the trap of believing your life isn't interesting. Thankfully, Mark Leruste is here to show us otherwise. In *Glow In The Dark*, Mark shows us the power of a life story – and how everyone sharing that story with people in a genuine and authentic way can be one of the most transformative things for your life and business.'

Mike Pacchione, celebrity speech coach and host of Best Speech podcast

'Mark practices what he preaches and is living proof that sharing your story can catapult a career to new heights. His compelling arguments and relevant examples will spark ideas and have you scribbling down copious notes of what to do! Mark has been on the journey himself and his insights are insanely valuable. The methods in this book will get you out of the shadows and into the spotlight where you belong.'

Jodie Cook, Entrepreneur and author of *Ten Year Career*

'Lots of people tell you that you need to have a story when presenting. Not everyone tells you how to do it though. Mark leads by example and *Glow In The Dark* is a blueprint of not just the WHY but the HOW.'

David McQueen, Co-Founder of Q Square Ltd

'Everyone loses when bright people play small. Mark Leruste brilliantly changes the dream killing question, "Who do you think you are?" to "Who do you think you are to NOT share your story?" This book is must-read for anyone seeking to have not only an authentic business – but an authentic life.'

Valerie Young, author of *The Secret Thoughts of Successful Women* and Co-Founder of the Impostor Syndrome Institute

# Glow In The Dark

*How Sharing Your Personal Story
Can Transform Your Business and
Change Your Life*

## MARK LERUSTE

JOHN
MURRAY
LEARNING

First published in Great Britain by John Murray Learning in 2022
An imprint of John Murray Press
A division of Hodder & Stoughton Ltd,
An Hachette UK company

1

A CIP catalogue record for this title is available from the British Library

Trade Paperback ISBN 978 1 529 39892 2
eBook ISBN 978 1 529 39894 6

Typeset by KnowledgeWorks Global Ltd.

Printed and bound in Great Britain by Clays Ltd, Elcograf S.p.A.

John Murray Press policy is to use papers that are natural, renewable and
recyclable products and made from wood grown in sustainable forests.
The logging and manufacturing processes are expected to conform
to the environmental regulations of the country of origin.

John Murray Press
Carmelite House
50 Victoria Embankment
London EC4Y 0DZ

www.johnmurraypress.co.uk

For Sophie and Louis,
May your lives be full of stories worth sharing.

# Contents

# Preface

In October 2012 I found myself facing a small group of people in a dodgy, grungy bar in the middle of Paris surrounded
by tired rock-n-roll-themed memorabilia on the walls, the
stench of stale beer rising from the floor, and equipped with
nothing more than a laptop and a questionable moustache.

My mission was simple: launch the very first official campaign in France of Movember, a global event organised by
The Movember Foundation that raises awareness and funds
for men's health by getting men to grow a moustache and
effectively turn themselves into a Freddy Mercury lookalike
for thirty days.

As I launched into my enthusiastic pitch, I remembered
what Bill, my manager, had told me during my on-boarding
process as Movember Team Europe employee number three:
*Don't worry about the money or how much you raise. Focus on
the fun, and the funds will follow.* Bill hadn't counted on the
French, who are notoriously resistant to making fun of themselves (or experiencing any sense of joy for that matter ... and
I say this with love as someone who is half French).

Towards the end of my inaugural speech I saw a hand
in the crowd. It was a journalist who had been invited by
Isabelle, our PR contact, to help spread the word. 'That all
sounds great Mark, but what made *you* want to join Movember and launch the foundation in France?' the journalist asked.

I was taken by surprise. I mean sure, we had received
some media training back at Movember HQ, but I hadn't

thought about the most basic question of all: why had *I* left a perfectly great, stable and reputable job at a leading business school in my hometown, a job that came with many perks, to join a hairy charity that gets men to grow lip blankets?

In that moment I knew I had a decision to make.

Up until then, my personal and professional lives were two separate entities that absolutely needed to be and remained apart.

But I also remembered how I'd felt when I went through a really bad patch back in 2009 when, after a bad break-up, I quit my corporate job and travelled halfway around the world to live at my parents' place. It was a struggle just to get out of bed.

How having no idea what I was going to do or which direction I should take left me feeling hopeless and, dare I say, depressed.

Until, that is, I came across a post that Tom, my cousin's husband, had posted on Facebook, sharing a ridiculous photo of his upper lip, talking about how he was growing a moustache in November for a charity called Movember.

After clicking through the link to the foundation's website I saw images, branding and messages that spoke to me, especially as a young man. It was fun, edgy, and more importantly, it was all for a good cause.

'Having fun, doing good' was splashed across the website. That's all I needed to hear.

So I signed up, thoroughly clean-shaven, and started asking friends, family and colleagues for donations. For the first time in a long time I experienced a sense of hope and belonging. I had something to look forward to.

But shy of a handful of very close people, pretty much no one knew that I had recently gone through a rough patch, that I had struggled in silence and was afraid to let anybody else know how I felt, let alone tell a journalist from a major newspaper about it in front of a live crowd.

Yet here I was, needing to give this eager journalist an answer. Naturally, my mind went racing: 'Okay, Mark, are you going to bullshit this journalist just to be safe? Or are you going to take a leap of faith, be real and risk it for a chocolate biscuit?'

Up until that point I had always chosen the safer path. But for some reason, as I connected to why I was there and how I'd ended up on that stage, for the first time, instead of giving a surface-level answer, I told the truth.

I shared why I had personally felt drawn to join the foundation by telling my story of struggle behind closed doors, of not knowing who to turn to, of feeling guilty for feeling that way, given my extreme place of privilege, and that this was why I was excited to launch and grow the Movember campaign in France and beyond. Aside from myself, I had met other men who struggled to take care of themselves and talk about their mental health, so surely there were others like us who needed to know that they were not alone.

I'm not going to lie: it was scary as hell. I felt exposed and naked. But I also knew that there was a reason I was drawn to this role, to Movember's mission to spread the message that talking saves lives.

As I wrapped up my story, something remarkable happened. None of the consequences I'd imagined would result from opening up publicly about things I had always thought to be 'shameful', 'unlovable' or 'unworthy' materialised. The Earth didn't open up and swallow me in a dark abyss, and the audience didn't throw rotten tomatoes. Thank God!

After I ended my talk and answered a few more questions, Jeremy, a young man in the crowd who had heard about the event through social media, thanked me for opening up about my own struggles. He, too, had been going through a bad patch, and this was the first time he felt like he wasn't alone. He wasn't too sure about this whole growing a *mo* (Australian slang for moustache) Movember thing before coming, but now, he told me, he was 100 per cent going to sign up and take part in the campaign, and he'd get a bunch of his friends to join in, too.

I was blown away.

Instead of rejection, I got connection. From shame to service, I went from striving for applause to working for a cause.

In that moment I understood that when it comes to business or non-profit, people need to trust you and to feel seen, heard and understood in order to want to do business with you.

And nothing achieves that outcome faster than being honest about your story and sharing why you do what you do.

From 2012 to 2016 I shared Movember's story and talked about why I was so passionate about growing the foundation's mission across Europe more times than I can remember, easily thousands of times across hundreds of companies and organisations. The more I shared it, the more comfortable I became, the better my story landed, and the more engaged people were. I started noticing patterns: when people were paying attention; when they were drifting off; when I'd get a laugh, a sigh or a reaction.

It taught me that a great story isn't written, a great story is honed, and it sharpens as you share it.

The result? My manager, Bill, was right. I never had to focus on the money. Sure I mentioned the need to raise funds, as it was an important part of our objectives and call-to-action, but instead of making it *all* about the money I simply connected with, enrolled and engaged my audience with a powerful story that left a lasting impact.

Never could I have imagined that having the courage to share and connect my personal story to the story behind the charity, and daring to share it publicly, would lead to my team raising over €2.8 million for men's health and enrolling 110,000 fundraisers to sign up, winning multiple awards along the way.

Never could I have imagined that sharing Movember's story thousands of times would lead to me being invited to talk about the work we did on *Le Petit Journal* (a French television programme often compared to *The Daily Show* with Trevor Noah) with Yann Barthès in front of an audience of 1.2 million people.

Your story can do the same for you and your audience.

Imagine sharing your story – the story of your life or the story of your business – in public. It might be on a major stage or an influential podcast, with a client or in front of your team. Imagine that instead of feeling nervous, scared, ashamed or uncertain, you felt excited, clear and super-confident in your ability to inspire, engage and enrol your audience with your life-changing story.

Now imagine that your story – the one you've taken time to unpack and have the courage to share publicly – has a ripple effect around the world. You're getting messages and emails from total strangers thanking you for sharing it. Imagine, instead of having to chase business, people are actively reaching out to work with you and for you.

This isn't wishful thinking or a lofty dream. This is something that you absolutely can and will achieve if you have the courage to show up, read this book, and do the work.

'I believe that there's something interesting about anyone and everyone, you just have to figure out what that something is.'

Tony Hsieh, author of *Delivering Happiness* and former Zappos CEO

# Welcome

- Are you tired of worrying what other people think of you?

- Are you fed up with hiding behind your business?

- Do you struggle to introduce yourself and your business when it matters?

- Do you want to build a better connection with your audience?

- Do you have an innate desire to be more authentic and engaging with your content?

- Would you like to get over the mental barriers that erode your confidence when you share your story in public?

If you answered yes to any of the above then you're in good company. These are common problems; most of us have them, and thousands of talented entrepreneurs and business leaders self-sabotage their impact, play small, and hide behind their businesses because of them. Be it shying away from talking about the great work that they do, running away from speaking opportunities or resenting having to be on social media, they're simply too afraid of what people might think or say if they showed up as their authentic selves in public and shared their true stories. And fear of being criticised, butterflies in the stomach, being scared of rejection and humiliation mean that countless brilliant ideas and movements will never see the light of day because their creators are too timid to be themselves and share them.

What if I told you that you could learn a practical and safe way to get comfortable with being yourself in public, to accept who you are, and to celebrate every part of you and your story, even the scary bits? What if I told you there's a way to muzzle your inner critic and silence that voice that tells you you aren't good enough, smart enough or successful enough? What if I told you there's a method to connect with people on a deeper level, and to embrace your story, warts and all, to the point where sharing it becomes effortless? What if I told you that your story is special enough that others will *ask* you to tell it? What if I told you that you could learn to do this with confidence, authority and authenticity? And what if I told you that this skill can help you to substantially increase your income, impact and influence?

No matter where you are on life's journey, no matter what your experience or background, you can learn a simple framework to turn your myriad experiences into a powerful, engaging and clear *origin story* that people will connect with, remember and want to share with others on your behalf. This book will tell you how to do it.

## The Problem and the Solution

I've spent the best part of the last decade solving a puzzle: What stops most people from having the impact, income and influence they desire?

Every industry has a group of entrepreneurs and leaders it really admires, who are authentic, engaging and who inspire others when they share their stories, be it on stage, in the press, on the phone, on social media or in a team meeting. These are people who we really *want* to listen to, and follow, and work with and for. And although we can see with our own eyes and hear with our own ears that it's possible to *be* this sort of leader, we still don't feel like we belong in their group – the group that includes the engaging, inspiring and authentic leaders we see on television and read about in books.

For me, Scott Harrison, founder and CEO of charity: water comes to mind. Despite a questionable past living a full-on hedonistic lifestyle in New York City, spending a decade surviving on drugs, alcohol, sex and parties, being emotionally and spiritually bankrupt and requiring the external validation of others, Scott managed to turn his life around after a trip to post-war Liberia in 2004. This led him to launch charity: water, a non-profit organisation that brings clean and safe drinking water to people in developing countries, raising $101 million in 2021.[1]

What inspires me the most isn't just the impact Scott's non-profit organisation has had, but how Scott has found a way to fully own his past, warts and all; how he is unafraid to share it every time he talks on stage, is interviewed on a podcast or is featured in the media. The result: his non-profit has attracted some of the best talent and raised millions of dollars for a great cause.

Seeing Scott share his story so openly, in public, gives me and hopefully you, too, the permission to fully own your story.

I'm here to tell you that you absolutely *do* belong in that group too. The truth is that most of us, including massively successful businesspeople and influencers, don't think we have histories worth sharing. We think we're mundane, boring, inconsequential, *dull*. You might think so, but you've spent your whole life living with yourself. The rest of us don't know you. And sharing your authentic self means distilling that essence of who you are into a *message* or a *story* that will tell the tale of exactly how you got where you are. Do you think Sir Paul McCartney has stories worth sharing? How about Oprah Winfrey? Their willingness to share their authentic selves provides a road map to their success. They tell us how they reached their destinations. You are no different.

I know you aren't Paul McCartney or Oprah Winfrey. Neither am I. But let me tell you something. One of the things that makes successful people *successful* is their willingness to share their authentic selves. It creates trust, confidence, empathy, admiration and a perception of authority and expertise that can't be built in any other way. This authentic openness, and a refusal to hide behind a facade, doesn't just tell us *how* people such as Paul McCartney and Oprah Winfrey achieved their success; it is, to a large extent, exactly *why* they became successful. 'But what about their talent?' you ask. I'm not discounting their talent, but talent isn't everything. Do you like Paul McCartney's music? Maybe. Do you like *Paul McCartney*? Perhaps. Regardless of how you feel about him or his music, know that there are millions of people who do like him. So why? Beatlemania wasn't all about music. It was about four people who didn't hide who they were, who generously shared their authentic selves with the world. It worked.

Oprah Winfrey is a great interviewer and TV host. We have no shortage of people who are good at those things. So what sets Oprah apart? Although you may not know what the exact answer is, my guess is you've felt it. Oprah has been open about her difficult childhood, from growing up poor to being sexually abused; she hasn't held back from sharing her true authentic story. It turns out that sharing her authentic self has worked out pretty well for her, hasn't it?

I'll show you how to make this happen for *you*. Your business can be more fun, more profitable, easier to manage and, more importantly, you'll finally get to be 100 per cent *you* in the process.

That's right. Despite the popular advice of *fake it until you make it*, despite feeling like you have to put up a front to appear as intelligent or successful as the other people in the room, I'm here to tell you that you don't have to waste any more time or energy trying to be someone you're not. Hiding behind your business is the last thing the world needs. The truth is, when you learn to stop hiding your true self, when you find the courage to put yourself out there more authentically, on your own terms, your business will expand and elevate in ways that you cannot even imagine. It's when a struggling business begins to thrive, when an anonymous entrepreneur becomes a household name, and when someone who impacts the lives in their neighbourhood becomes a force for good throughout the world.

- Imagine clients lining up to do business with you

- Imagine having top talent dying to work with you

- Imagine growing an engaged and loyal audience who want to see you and your business succeed

- Imagine having influential media knocking on your door eager to share your story

This is what's possible when you embrace what you're about to learn.

In these pages you'll discover the tactics that have helped entrepreneurs and business leaders who knew they had more to offer, who wanted to inspire a bigger audience to have a bigger impact, who grew weary of playing a role instead of being themselves, and who were tired of being the best-kept secret, lessons that have helped those same entrepreneurs and business leaders produce extraordinary results.

*Spoiler alert*: The transformational journey you're about to embark upon will require you to find the courage to own and tell your story to your audience, authentically and truthfully, warts and all. It won't necessarily be easy, but it will be worth it, and I'll be here to guide you along every bend in the path.

## You Do You

If you see two versions of yourself in the mirror, the professional you and the private you, and you're always hiding parts of the private you in business, this book will help you realise that not only can the two halves of yourself be united into an integrated whole, but they absolutely *should* be integrated. *Being yourself is good for business.* In fact, being yourself is the only way to be truly free, to reach your full potential and to live the life you want.

It's also the only way to be your most authentic self. The great news is that the more authentic your persona becomes, and the more it integrates with every aspect of your life, the more you'll raise your credibility, build a loyal audience, grow your business to new levels, and gain the peace of mind that comes with being yourself at all times and in all situations, including in the business sphere. Why does this work? Because people – all of us – can sense authenticity. We instinctively know when someone is being their authentic self, and we know when someone isn't. We're attracted to authenticity. Authenticity is magnetic. Authenticity is *essential*.

This book is for the brave leaders who need to raise their profile to attract their ideal clients, but who don't like to put themselves out there, who fly underneath the radar or who simply don't know where to start.

This book is for those who know deep down they're really good at what they do, who care deeply about their work, but who struggle to brag about themselves.

This book is for those who know they can provide value to those they work with, and deliver outstanding results for their clients and customers, but who shy away from the spotlight because they're too comfortable hiding behind their business and playing small.

This book is for those who want to become influencers and connectors, who want to inspire large numbers of people, and who want to feel comfortable being themselves on stage or behind a microphone.

This book is for those who need the courage to be imperfect in public.

This book is for those who, when they *do* take a step forward, feel like impostors, like they are not being their true selves.

Finally, this book is for those who know enough is enough and who are ready to change once and for all, so they, too, can inspire others on their journeys.

Let's face it, chances are, you picked up this book because you want to engage, enlist and inspire others without feeling uncomfortable with yourself, without worrying what others might think, without being judged and criticised, and without pretending to be someone you're not.

It's time to level up and become the inspiring and engaging leader you know you can be. You have it within yourself to be more than you let the world see. It's time to show up as your effortless self, give your full potential the best shot possible, and stop living your life with the handbrake on.

Too many people feel as though they must wear a mask when walking through the front door of their office, as if the only way to fit in and be accepted is to play small and hide the core parts of who they are. The price we pay is waking up feeling like we are living a lie and robbing those around us of our impact.

It's time we put an end to the painful process of feeling like you have to be one person at work and another at home.

It's time to end the idea that your story doesn't matter.

Your story *does* matter. In fact, it's the missing piece you've been looking for all along.

## Glow in the Dark

The sad truth is that *most* of us hide behind a mask, and when we switch between work and home we swap one mask for another. It's tiring, it saps your energy and it takes a toll on your mental health. People who have learned to drop the mask and be their authentic selves under all circumstances shine like beacons in the dark. They're happier, more care-free and unafraid to share their passions with the world. We're attracted to them without even understanding why. As you work through this book you, too, will learn to glow in the dark, to be a lighthouse to all those who are burdened by the need to present a false front to the world. You will become the lighthouse that guides your audience to a safe harbour. And when you've mastered the skills, it will be *effortless*.

## Let the Transformational Journey Begin

If you're ready to take the first step towards learning how to be more inspiring and engaging with your words or work, if you're ready to step outside of the shadows and start having the impact you want, and if you're ready to be your most authentic self in every situation, especially when it matters, then get ready for the ride.

Because one thing is for sure. If you read this book and apply its lessons, if you keep an open mind and are ready to be coached, and if you can overcome the resistance that we all experience when we try to level up, then your world will become a very different place, a place filled with more potential and opportunity than you could possibly imagine.

*I can't wait.*

# Introduction: Unlock the Superpower Within

The doors finally opened and we made our way down a narrow, dark staircase flanked by neon lights. We descended to the basement and picked our way through tight rows of plastic chairs waiting for brave pundits to take their seats.

We were at a buzzing underground comedy club outside Johannesburg, South Africa, and I was about to experience my first live stand-up comedy. The MC took the stage, grabbed the mic, and introduced the comedians. One by one, a wide range of talented entertainers did their best to make us pee our pants. Behind the laughter, though, I realised a fundamental truth: *a good comedian is comfortable talking about themselves in public.* The most compelling comedians would effortlessly (or so it seemed) share their most embarrassing shortcomings, flaws and failures, along with thoughts and opinions that no one should say out loud. *Ever.* Turning their dirty little secrets into their greatest asset for connection.

It was as if they were breaking the cardinal rule, 'Thou shalt not talk about the ugly bits.' And yet here they were, using their darkest secrets as material. And it worked. The crowd loved it.

But what I left with that night wasn't just a new-found love for live stand-up comedy. I left with a new obsession born of a nagging question that wouldn't leave me alone: Why can some people own their shit, share it publicly and feel no shame about it, while others (like me) would rather die than share 'the truth' about who we really are?

I felt as though there was no way I could talk about all the parts of me that I was deeply ashamed or embarrassed about, and yet I knew in my bones that there was clearly a way to overcome those fears and fully own all of me.

Of course, I also understood the argument that it's not ready until it's ready. That sometimes these things take time or that people would rather keep parts of themselves private. But I also learned in that moment the liberating feeling of letting go of what we deem to be shameful about our past or who we are.

In fact, it was around that moment that I was reminded of an epic rap battle in the movie *8 Mile* in which the main character, B-Rabbit, played by Eminem, is in the final round of a rap battle with his main rival, Papa Doc, played by Anthony Mackie. B-Rabbit goes first. For those who are unfamiliar with the protocols of rap battles, the goal is generally to make fun of, humiliate or 'diss' your opponent. But instead of leading with a barrage of insults, B-Rabbit instead leads with his flaws, broadcasting every problem, setback and humiliation he suffers, effectively disarming Papa Doc and leaving him speechless. B-Rabbit knew a simple truth: no one can hurt you when you have nothing to hide.

Fear and shame tend to vanish when they are brought into the light. If you're spending time trying to hide elements about you, you're operating from a place of defence. If you're able to get to a place where you have nothing to hide, or nothing brings you shame, then you can focus on the stuff that matters, be it living a more meaningful life or building an impactful business.

This phenomenon of being your effortless self on stage or in public is a *superpower* and it isn't reserved for stand-up comedians or hip-hop artists. I've seen this work for rock bands and, more importantly, for public speakers, founders and CEOs of forward-thinking companies.

At TEDxHackney back in August 2012, just a few months after moving to London from France, I heard an inspiring speaker named Femi Edmund Adeyemi, the founder of NTS Radio, a global radio platform broadcasting music from over fifty cities around the globe, live 24/7. Femi told of how he went from being stuck in a job he didn't like, to quitting his job to pursue his passion, to being homeless and sleeping on his friend's couch while he started his movement on the airwaves i.e. giving a voice to the voiceless by leveraging digital broadcasting technology. 'Ultimately you have a choice to make,' he said, 'either you want financial stability in a job you're not fulfilled in or financial insecurity chasing your dream and passion.'[2]

Although I can see how much more challenging this could be had he had a family to support, I was inspired by his story, and especially by his ability to just be himself on stage. He seemed effortless on stage. His energy was grounded. He didn't seem as though he needed to impress anyone or need our validation to feel as though his message mattered. And when I thanked him afterwards, I was surprised to find he was the same person off stage as he was on. It was refreshing.

As a child, I was told that there are things we talk about at home that are not okay to talk about in public, or even

outside of our nuclear family, from family secrets to fart-
ing jokes. Additionally, a deep sense of inadequacy born of
being bullied by my teachers at school for being dyslexic
meant that I always thought I had to pretend to be smarter
than I was, that I had to separate the real me from the school
me. So seeing someone who had somehow found a way to
marry all of themselves when in a public and professional
setting, unafraid to publicly air setbacks and failures, was
mind-blowing. It wasn't something I knew or believed was
possible, and yet here it was. Right in front of me.

When I started working with Sarah, a founding managing
director of a seven-figure company, she told me, 'I absolutely
love hearing other people's stories and I'm super empathetic
towards them. What informed them and drove them to this
amazing thing they created. I see an example of that, and I
think, *"Why can't I do that? Why can't I have less care for
what everyone else thinks?"'*

What happens when we let go of the fear of opening
up? It's rarely the pain, rejection and certain death that we
expect. Instead, what we often find is connection, acceptance and healing. Believe me, I know how counter-intuitive
that may sound. But soon you'll understand and experience
what I mean.

The ability to show up as your effortless, authentic self in
business and life is not reserved for a lucky few or for the
crazy ones who simply don't care what people think. No. It's
available to all of us. It's available to *you*.

Think about it. The energy it takes to hold back, to play
small, to hide, to be who everyone else wants you to be, to
play the leader, to control every element of what the world
sees and knows about you, is exhausting. What else could
you do with that energy? You could connect with, enlist,

inspire, empower, elevate and impact others. It also makes it easier to highlight the things that matter to you, the causes you support, the business you wish to promote, and the people you want to lift up (see, it isn't all about you!). And that's just for starters.

The world needs to see the *real you*, not just the highly curated part of you. It's time to fall in love with being seen, being more visible as the real you, and sharing your story, because the world is starved of truth.

# Hack Your Human Operating System

The fear of being exposed, of being seen, of being visible is often pegged to the fear of being rejected, judged, made fun of or ostracised. Fear of being cast out from the pack is primal, and we are hard-wired to avoid things that could cause us to be isolated, things like telling stories that could be painful or embarrassing. So when you feel that pang of reluctance in your gut, just think, you're tapping into your deepest simian roots. It's part of our *human operating system*.

Deep stuff, I know, but it's true.

But this also means you aren't alone. We all feel this fear. We are biologically designed to fit in and not stand out, with deep neural programming that tells us that belonging to the group is essential to our very survival. Anyone who broke away from the pack risked being left alone in the wild, stranded, having to fend for themselves against predators and the elements.

We no longer live in the primeval world, but the fear remains. In her book *Everything Is Figureoutable* (2019), Marie Forleo shares a story about Bruce Springsteen and how he understands that no matter how long he's been performing in front of live crowds, he always feels a sense of fear and stress before going on stage. Somewhere in the back of Bruce's mind there's an ape telling him not to go out on that stage because he might fail and be cast out of the group. But Bruce has hacked his human operating system. He knows that the fear he feels is his body's signal telling him he's ready to rock and roll. As it turns out, whether we feel fear or excitement, the physical manifestations are basically identical. Our pulse gets faster, our mouth goes dry, our palms get sweaty and we feel all sorts of feelings with an overwhelming internal message screaming '*Stop!* You're not safe!'.

And yet ... When you step out on the stage, real or meta-phorical, that's when greatness happens. In this book we'll talk about ways to overcome these fears, because the alternative is *invisibility*.

# Invisibility Is a Superpower, but in Business It's Kryptonite

*I don't know why people are so keen to put the details of their private life in public; they forget that invisibility is a superpower.*

Banksy

Banksy has a point. I mean, he has built his entire career on being incognito. And the Cloak of Invisibility came in handy for Harry Potter too. But usually, if you're in business, invisibility isn't a superpower. It's kryptonite. If we don't know about you, how can we do business with you? Sure, we can do business with people we don't know. I doubt you know who leads your bank. But the truth is, for the vast majority of us, obscurity isn't a luxury we can afford.

If invisibility is kryptonite, then raising your profile is the antidote. That's why it's so important to find the courage to amplify who you are, and to share your story clearly and authentically, in public. If you want to impact the world with your message, experience what it feels like to be your authentic self with others, and attract people (and a bigger audience), the ability to comfortably share your authentic story is crucial. If you want business to chase you and opportunities to find you, then it's time to put yourself out there, to step up, unpack and share your story.

Even better, your story is the only thing other people can't copy. They can sell your products and provide your services, but they can't be *you*. You, and your authentic story, are an insurance policy, because your mission emerged from your story, from your history, and it's yours alone. It belongs to no one else.

In case you haven't noticed by now, I believe telling your story matters.

For over a decade I have coached and helped founders, entrepreneurs and business leaders to find their purpose and share their stories, from unpacking and clarifying their messages to communicating them with confidence both publicly and privately. The results they've achieved from sharing their genuine, authentic stories have been *mind-blowing*. Armed with their new courage, they have gone on to give TEDx talks with over a million views, they have raised seven-figure sums from angel investors, they have launched number one Apple podcasts, they have won prestigious awards in their industries, and they have been featured on television and in the national press. They've even secured major book deals.

But the transformation didn't just happen with their businesses; it happened with their personal lives, too. The more confident they became, the more purpose-driven they felt, and the more easily they were able to connect with others on a much deeper level.

There's one more unexpected consequence of owning and sharing your story authentically. Those who learn this skill report feeling as though a heavy burden has been lifted from their shoulders, and, for the first time, they feel at home being themselves, without a facade and without pretence. It's liberating.

As Caitlin McNamara, who curated the first Hay Literary Festival in Abu Dhabi and who, despite the possible backlash, went public about her alleged rape by an Emirati royal, said to a *Guardian* reporter, 'For me, the moment I spoke publicly about what had happened a huge weight was lifted. All of that fear and fury just dissipated by shining a spotlight on what happened.'[3]

## 'Okay Mark, But I'm Just Not Built That Way'

The biggest mistake I hear people make is believing someone is either born with the gift of personality and charisma, or they're not.

I'm here to burst that bubble with all my might, and tell you that it's not some magical gift only a select few of us are born with.

Everyone can learn how to engage and inspire their audience with their story, as long as they're willing to be honest, real and brave in the process.

Like any skill, this can be taught, learned, practised, even mastered.

That's why I'm so excited for you to be here. If you're here it means you want to make a difference. If you want to learn how to capture the imaginations and hearts of your ideal audience, if you want to learn how to become more honest and compelling when speaking in public, and if you're looking to become the kind of person people pay attention to and whose opinions are sought and respected, you've come to the right place.

If you're tired of reading every self-help book and sitting through endless courses, you've come to the right place. Because my promise is that if you dare to trust the process I'm about to share with you, if you have the courage to show up fully, then this book will be a game changer.

Both for your business and for your personal life.

*The question is, are you in?*

*Excellent! Your journey begins on the next page.*

# How to Use This Book

**Part One: Why Your Story Is Your Secret Weapon to Success** introduces you to why stories matter and, more particularly, why your story matters. Despite what you may think or feel, your personal story, your origin story, is the secret ingredient of your success, especially when it comes to connecting and engaging with your audience – whether it's the public or your employees – in a powerful and meaningful way that makes people want to work with you.

**Part Two: How to Unleash Your Story** reveals the tools and techniques that many well-known business leaders and celebrities instinctively understand. You will learn exactly how to unpack, shape, structure and share any life event in a way that makes people sit up, pay attention, remember who you are and connect with what you have to say or share.

# PART 1

# Why Your Story Is Your Secret Weapon to Success

To get the most out of your reading experience, be sure to evaluate yourself at the beginning of your journey, before reading the rest of this book, and check your progress and acknowledge your transformation at the end of it by filling out your Growth Assessment at www.GlowInTheDarkBook. com/growth

# CHAPTER ONE

# Hello, My Name Is Impostor

On 31 December 2014 I received an email from Nick Kershaw, founder and CEO of Impact Marathon Series, telling me that I had been selected as one of the 50 Most Inspiring People in London. I was sure the organisers had made a mistake.

When I saw a small sample list of the other selected members I thought to myself, there's no way I'm meant to be in that group of people!

I was in the company of people who had rowed across the Atlantic for charity, skateboarded across Australia, climbed some of the world's highest peaks, and run across New Zealand. Why was I up there with all these incredibly inspiring game changers?

According to the organisers, I deserved to be on that list, but I just didn't see how what I had done (helped raise awareness and funds for men's health, coached and supported impact-driven entrepreneurs, launched a plant-based protein smoothie company in seven days with £100, etc.), even compared to the achievements of everyone else on that list. I simply saw what I had achieved as 'less than' the rest of the nominees.

This experience of feeling like a fraud wasn't new to me. After all, impostor syndrome is something I've been intimately aware of, and in bed with, since my early years of struggling to spell or read aloud in class, hearing my classmates laugh at the humiliating jokes about my many spelling mistakes inflicted by my teachers. This dreaded, gut-wrenching feeling that I am about to be caught by the fraud squad, that at any time someone is going to come and let me know there's been a huge mistake, and ask me to give back all the great things in my life, is something I know all too well.

As I sat there in the audience on launch night, listening to *truly* inspiring and unconventional people like Sophie Radcliffe, Dave Cornthwaite and Julia Immonen, all accomplished (and slightly crazy) adventurists, talk about their experiences, I kept on thinking, the organisers clearly made a mistake.

As the evening went on, I saw the names of others on the list – Danny Bent (founder of Project Awesome and One Run), Leon McCarron (award-winning writer and explorer), Anna McNuff (bestselling author and one of Condé Nast Traveller's '50 most influential travellers of our time') and Sean Conway (endurance adventurer and first person to cycle, swim and run the length of Great Britain) – only to then see my name and face appear on the slide deck in front of the entire live audience. Now would be the moment that everyone would turn towards me, point their fingers and laugh.

That didn't happen.

The funny thing was, for the ceremony, I had invited my parents and a small group of friends and clients to join me. Should the fraud squad kick down the door and storm towards me, I could at least say, surely anyone with an entourage is important enough to be featured on some kind of list, right? That, and maybe walking in as a group, would make me look a little less out of place. At least that's what I hoped.

But here's when everything changed for me. To my big surprise, I was fascinated to hear that almost everyone I spoke to who was nominated and selected to be part of this group of inspiring people felt the exact same way as me – what the hell am I doing here? And some saw *me* as someone they weren't worthy of sharing a list with. It was mind-blowing.

The more I heard how baffled everyone was by their inclusion on this list, the more I thought everyone needed to hear these voices inside the heads of some of the most inspiring, influential and impactful people in one of the world's greatest cities.

I mean, I had been on the receiving end of similar doubts, but for the first time I experienced them in a public way by sharing them with others who, in turn, shared their own experiences with me.

A day or two later I emailed the other members asking them if they'd be up for coming on my brand new, nameless, yet to be launched podcast to talk about their journeys and to share their stories. My mission was simple. I wanted to create a safe space for candid conversations about the things most people don't usually get to hear in public; honest, vulnerable and real conversations about what it really takes to go after your passion, live your purpose and turn your message into a movement.

My intention was also to provide an alternative to the typical highly curated, surface-level podcast conversations, where everyone seems to be doing great and living the perfect life or running the ideal business. I wanted to share the less than perfect reality behind the scenes, so that people could see they're not alone in their struggle to make an impact. I wanted to create the bridge between two worlds, the world of 'I suck' and the world of 'I'm successful'. To change the narrative, to shift the story being told around what it takes to be on the other side of inspiring. We all need to hear about the struggles beneath the success. As you'll hear me say over and over, we're all the same, we're all human at our core.

# Lessons from the Front Line of Impact

Since 2015 I have hosted a podcast called 'The Unconventionalists' in which I interview unconventional world-class leaders from across the fields of business, politics, advocacy, sport, journalism and the arts, who dare to be different and who found a way to carve their own path and challenge the status quo. I realised two things pretty quickly.

First, the people I was interviewing on my show and the people I was coaching in my spare time (typically unfulfilled professionals and frustrated entrepreneurs looking to do more meaningful work) weren't that different. Both groups were made up of genuinely good-hearted and good-natured people who cared and wanted to make a difference and do work that felt meaningful and fulfilling. Both groups also struggled with bouts of self-doubt.

The difference, however, was that one group (my podcast guests) were able to keep marching forward despite these feelings and limiting beliefs, while the other group (clients) felt paralysed, stuck in the starting blocks, because of how they perceived themselves, how they believed they should feel or who they thought they should become. As Dr Valerie Young, co-founder of the Impostor Syndrome Institute, told me, 'Feelings are the last thing to change.'

Second, given an opportunity, anyone can learn how to work through their fears, to be themselves and share their story in order to create an emotional connection with their audience. Which, in turn, helps attract positive media stories, gets you invited on to bigger stages, and acts as an ideal client or talent magnet.

The more I interviewed guests on my podcast and helped them unpack and share their stories and journeys with the world, the more I saw the impact it had both on the people I was working with and on the audience that was listening.

That's when I started being approached by founders, CEOs, entrepreneurs and business leaders, asking me to help them learn how to unpack their story so the world listens. They too had been hiding behind their business, grappling with some level of self-doubt or feelings that kept them stuck in the starting blocks. Even these phenomenally successful people suffered from impostor syndrome.

Since launching my podcast 'The Unconventionalists' (which won the best interview podcast category at the Podcasting for Business Awards 2021 #humblebrag), I've been fortunate enough to sit across from some incredibly inspiring people who, if you asked them, would tell you they consider themselves to be *unexceptional*.

Over years of researching and obsessing over what keeps talented entrepreneurs, founders and business owners from impacting the world with their message, one central question keeps coming up. Why are some leaders able to galvanise so much interest in what they do just by showing up and sharing what they're passionate about, while others hide in the shadows and are resistant to stepping into the limelight to talk about what they do, and duly struggle to gain any traction?

The answer boils down to two things:

**Number one**: The vast majority (maybe all) of the people I've interviewed who found a way to reach their definition of success are just as riddled with self-doubt, fear and insecurity as everyone else is. The difference is how they relate to those feelings.

Instead of letting themselves be paralysed by these fears, they learn to live with them and work through them. They don't wait for them to magically disappear or change, because they understand that these feelings are actually a signal for what matters. That the louder they get, the closer they are to doing what's right and needed. In short, they expect these feelings of impostor syndrome, of doubts or fears, of resistance, to be part of the journey, and they have accepted them as unwanted guests on their road trip to impact. They understand that these feelings can't be destroyed, but they can be managed.

**Number two**: All inspiring leaders have a powerful origin story that they are willing to share. This may sound obvious, but from CEOs like Noah Kagan and Mike Michalowicz, to bestselling authors like Paul Jarvis and Sarah Knight to entrepreneurs like Danielle LaPorte and Chris Guillebeau, every one of my guests, whether well known or otherwise, has a compelling story to tell, even if they don't know it.

And what I've enjoyed more than anything is helping my guests and clients unpack their stories to find the hidden gems that somehow feel irrelevant or insignificant to them, and bring them up to the surface for the world to experience and connect with.

Turns out, as much as we may hate the idea of it, our imperfections are what make us more influential. People want to connect to real people, but it takes great courage to bring the mask down and lay aside the shield for the sake of connection with our audience. But I also know that it's easier said than done, so before we move on I need to address the elephant in the room.

## What Impostor Syndrome Is – and What It Is Not

Impostor syndrome, like many other labels, has been thrown around in the media and in conversation to the point that it's difficult to even comprehend what it really is.

In 1978, psychologists Pauline Rose Clance and Suzanne Imes defined the concept as *impostor phenomenon.* In a nutshell, it's the struggle to internalise and own our successes, talents or skills, and instead attribute our achievements to external forces. It's the inability to own our greatness, or the constant need to downplay our skills and give credit to others for our own success or achievements. It's as if a compliment was a hot potato, and as soon as someone throws it at you the only thing you want to do is get it out of your hands and throw it back or give it to someone else.

According to Jaruwan Sakulku's article 'The Impostor Phenomenon', published in the *Journal of Behavioral Science*,[4] it's estimated that 70 per cent of people experience impostor feelings at some point in their lives. That's a lot! And it's worse for entrepreneurs and business leaders. In the UK, a whopping 83 per cent of founders, CEOs and entrepreneurs have experienced these feelings.[5]

What I find fascinating is that many of the people I've spoken to or work with feel that impostor syndrome isn't what holds them back. They feel that they know they're good at what they do, and don't second guess their talents or achievements. They know they've got the goods. Rather, it's the fear of being judged by others that gets in their way. At least, that's what they *think*.

Both impostor syndrome and fear of judgement share the same room; both stem from a discomfort with being seen.

Now they (or you) may or may not experience impostor feelings, but what I've learned from talking to Dr Valerie Young, author of *The Secret Thoughts of Successful Woman* (2011) and co-founder of the Impostor Institute, who I mentioned earlier, is that playing small, i.e. flying under the radar and avoiding becoming more visible – *the fear of being judged* – can absolutely be part of the coping mechanism of dealing with impostor syndrome, because the less visible you are, the safer it is. If people can't see you then they can't call you out. You can't lose the game if you aren't playing.

Again, no matter how well someone may appear to have it all together, the vast majority of founders, entrepreneurs and business leaders struggle with some form of impostor syndrome.

In fact, I'd say it's often one of the driving forces that pushes so many of us to start a business, because deep down we want to prove to ourselves that we're enough, that we are lovable or worthy of love. I know, shit got deep, but it's true.

# The Many Manifestations of Impostor Syndrome

Expressed in many different ways, impostor syndrome manifests itself mostly through the inner dialogue that nobody gets to hear or see apart from ourselves. Of course, this may be a script that you adopted because of a traumatic event or because of something someone once told you. I know that's the case for me. I can still hear the words being spat at me as a child, coming from my angry (and, let's face it, bitter) French school teachers telling me how useless I was and how I'd never accomplish anything in life because of my inability to pay attention, do maths, read out loud or spell correctly.

You may recognise a few of these sentences that have been shared with me over the years by hundreds of founders, entrepreneurs and business leaders.

- 'Who am I to talk about this?'

- 'It's all been said and done, what do I have to add?'

- 'There are people who are far more qualified / able / better than me / etc.'

- 'Nobody cares about what I have to say, so why bother?'

- 'I will run out of things to say.'

- 'I'm going to make a fool of myself.'

- 'Nobody cares about my story.'

- 'What if I freeze and trip on my words?'

- 'What if I make a mistake and can't take it back?'

- 'What if I sound / look / come across as an idiot?'

- 'I don't want to hurt people involved in my story.'

- 'What if I get trolled online?'

Now if you're reading this and find yourself nodding because you can recognise yourself in there, you are not alone.

Here's an exercise I sometimes do when I run live workshops or give keynotes. *Write down the number one fear that gets in the way of you putting yourself and your story out there more.* I then get everyone to fold their paper and pass it around a couple of times. Then I ask everyone to open the paper they hold in their hands at the same time.

Let me tell you, every time I've done this exercise people laugh, smile or somehow get a sense of relief. Then I ask who is holding an answer that isn't theirs but which they can identify with or relate to?

Awkward relief erupts, smiles spread across the room, and the vast majority of hands go up.

It turns out, as you'll learn in this book, virtually everyone faces these fears.

## It Takes a Little Perspective

When my friend Josh, co-founder of one of the coolest and most innovative sustainable plant-based supplement companies on the planet, reached out to me, I was excited. I knew just how much Josh had to offer to the world. He wanted to raise his profile a bit more and put himself out there to start building the next chapter of his business life. Despite his company having grown more than 200 per cent over the past few years, despite having built a huge core following, despite selling millions of products to over thirty different countries worldwide, nobody really knew who he was. And he wanted it that way, until now. Now, for the first time, he felt ready to stretch and put himself out there, not to become famous but rather to give back to the next generation of disruptive founders and entrepreneurs.

What struck me in our conversation was that, despite his incredible business success, Josh didn't think that what he had achieved was that special. 'I don't have this incredible thing that I've achieved like some people,' he told me. Naturally, I smiled.

I knew exactly where he was coming from. He struggled to see how his story was relevant (*spoiler alert:* it's always super relevant!), although, ironically, he hoped it would help others start something meaningful. 'How do I take what I have and make it relevant so I can share it with others in a compelling way?' he asked.

He'd come to the right place.

When it came down to it, Josh wanted to learn how to tell his story 'in a way that is more inspiring'. And what I learned from working with him was that no matter how successful we are, no matter how big or impactful our business may be, we all lack perspective on our journey because we're simply too close to it.

Josh knew that parts of his story might be able to help others. He also knew there were parts of his story he was comfortable sharing and some he wasn't. That's why taking the time to reflect on his journey, as well as on the lessons he learned along the way (both good and bad), was really important to setting him on his path to raise his profile and serve more people. As a result he launched a podcast and his own blog, as writing was always his preferred medium to connect with his community.

After our session I received a handwritten card from Josh which I have framed and hung on my office wall. It simply reads, *Thank you for the permission to dream big.* It reminds me of the importance of having someone who can remind us of just how much we have to offer each other when we get out of our own way.

I can't tell you how many times I've spoken to friends, clients or podcast guests who, on the outside, look like they have it all together, have accumulated significant wealth, grown a following and built a core team and a successful company, only to tell me that they feel totally out of their depth and are constantly winging it, hoping nobody else will notice. And sometimes getting that out in the open is the first step in dealing with those feelings.

# What about Performing Introverts and Situational Extroverts?

Many of my clients are CEOs and founders who identify as either *performing introverts* or *situational extroverts*. They are able to show up and 'perform' when needed, but it drains them and let's face it, they don't particularly enjoy doing it.

When I first thought about writing this book, I wanted to create something that would help solve impostor syndrome for entrepreneurs who know they need to get out there more but hate the idea of doing it. I couldn't bear hearing countless stories of talented people who were really good at what they did, who were able to deliver outstanding value to their clients, but who weren't fulfilling their potential as leaders simply because of the story they told themselves about who they needed to become in order to have an impact.

In her bestselling book *Quiet: The Power of Introverts in a World That Can't Stop Talking* (2012), Susan Cain talks about the different ways people may resource themselves, i.e. how they rebuild their energy reserves. The idea is that where we get most of our energy from can help determine where we stand on the introvert–extrovert scale.

Introverts tend to wake up with ten tickets that represent all the energy they have for the day, and each interaction they have with people – when they find themselves having to do small talk or be in a crowded noisy environment – requires them to give up one of their tickets.

For each ticket they give up there will be a need to resource and retreat in order to replace that ticket. And if, by the end of the day, an introvert is left with few or no tickets then they can feel drained. Unsurprisingly, introverts often find refuge in quiet, isolation or silence.

Extroverts, on the other hand, tend to wake up with no tickets at all and get a ticket every time they interact with someone or do things that stimulate them, especially when they involve other people.

This is a gross generalisation of two extremes. Most of us can navigate and jump between both. For example, my partner Julie is probably more of an introvert and some of her favourite things in life are candles, quiet spaces and plans being cancelled. On the other hand, if Julie has to do public speaking or facilitation, she can, and she absolutely rocks it. It just means that afterwards she'll probably feel emotionally and physically drained and will need a few days to recharge. As for me, if I'm on my own for too long I start bouncing off the walls or fall into a deep depression. I get my energy from speaking to people and talking from a stage. I'm most at home when I get to interact and speak with others.

However, it's not all black and white. There are nuances, and we all dip in and out of the need for both ends of the spectrum. My brother, for example, is an ambivert. He needs a bit of both and can operate in both worlds. Even I need some quiet time, and since living with Julie I've come to appreciate the gifts of introverts and introversion.

No matter what you identify as, be it introvert, ambivert or extrovert, what you're about to learn applies to you too. This book is here to help you navigate the tricky waters of putting yourself out there when the idea of putting yourself out there sounds as much fun as haemorrhoids.

# What If You Could Unleash Your Superpower?

If you let me, I will show you how to unleash your superpower, no matter how scared you are of putting yourself out there or how much you feel like you are less than the person people think you are.

I've seen it over and over again with people I've worked with, whether I'm coaching CEOs on a one to one, running a workshop for clients, leading an accelerator for founders and business leaders, or delivering a keynote to an audience or organisation. The moment you give yourself permission to be your imperfect self in public is the moment you will experience a new level of confidence, fulfilment and impact beyond anything you have previously imagined.

When you dare to show up, when you find the courage to open up, when you've worked out your story, *then* your stories will take on lives of their own and people will start sharing them – *your stories* – with others, inspiring a whole new audience to join you on your quest.

Imagine what it would be like to have a constant flow of people knocking on your door dying to do business with you, who by the time they came to see you were already sold on who you are and what you stand for.

What if I told you that someone you were about to meet – be it at a job interview for a new role in your organisation, at a sales conversation with a major client or through a joint venture opportunity – was already emotionally engaged and invested in you and your mission because of the story you shared about why you do what you do?

That's the power of showing up as yourself and fully owning the power of your true story. It's the power of your *origin story*.

# CHAPTER TWO

# The Power of Being Authentic, Warts and All

On Friday, 16 December 2016, after reaching out to the organisers and jumping on a video call, I received an invitation to speak at TEDxCardiff. Naturally, I accepted. It was a dream come true, the realisation of a long-held ambition. I would finally take my place as part of one of the most prestigious speaking programmes of the twenty-first century. Strangely, I wasn't excited.

I was terrified.

I couldn't believe it. The dream I had nurtured for the past eight years, to talk on a TEDx stage, was finally going to become a reality, and there I was, dreading the prospect of stepping on stage to be seen and judged by the world. For the first time in my life I really felt a sense of fear at the idea of having to talk on stage, and failing in a really public way.

But I realised that it wasn't public speaking that I feared. By this point I had given hundreds, if not thousands, of public talks. I was comfortable in that environment. So what was I so afraid of?

It was the realisation that I couldn't hide.

That if I was going to take this TEDx talk seriously then I couldn't pretend to be someone I wasn't, and I certainly couldn't hide behind a mask. After all, the very construct of the event meant that you only had a limited amount of time to get your point across, and if you couldn't find a way to make it work, well, you were in for a rough eighteen minutes.

As far as I was concerned, I only had one shot at this. I saw it as a once-in-a-lifetime opportunity to deliver my most public talk to date, given the global audience and reach a TEDx talk can provide.

I wanted to make sure I did my very best to 'impress' when what I should have been aiming at was inspiring, empowering and serving others.

After wrestling for weeks around what talk I should give, I decided to go for one that would help people take action despite their resistance to do so. I wanted to address the misconception that what we need is clarity, when in fact what we need is trust. I wanted to share my belief that trusting in the process allows you to take action despite not knowing exactly where it will take you, and that big meaningful results can only come from taking a leap of faith.

And so I began a five-month process of researching, preparing, writing, agonising and practising my TEDx talk. At the time I thought the best method was to relentlessly practise my talk on every one of the twenty-one days leading up to the actual event, each time in front of a different friend, and ask for feedback.

Let me tell you, it was one of the most gruelling and emotionally draining experiences of my life.

Every day I'd hop on my bike or take the Tube to meet a friend somewhere in London and launch into my eighteen-minute monologue involving random stories, including a three-headed dragon metaphor, meant to represent our deepest fears which, looking back at it now, made no sense whatsoever. And every time I practiced my talk I was met with a blank stare and an open mouth.

'So what do you think?' I'd ask with a smile.

'... I mean, yeah. Well done. It's great that you're doing this. Wow! But, eh, I'm not quite sure about this three-headed dragon thing ...'

And every day I would get another list of notes and feed-back, crushing my soul little by little. But I kept going. I kept adapting my talk, implementing the feedback, and going back out again to test the new version.

Eventually, I discovered the real problem. I had created a talk that I thought was needed, or that I thought sounded smart, but it didn't include me. I hadn't poured myself into it. I hadn't shared anything personal. It was a talk that could have been given by anyone.

In short, it was a talk designed to be smart, not real.

## You Can Do Something Vanilla or You Can Do Something Real

I wasn't giving myself permission to be my authentic self, to be my *imperfect* self, in public. Instead of really opening up, I was hiding behind a three-headed dragon.

Until now, every talk I had given was purpose-built with a clear brief in mind, but this time I was asked to give a talk I really believed in and that could make a real change in people's lives.

Which, for some reason, made it scarier than anything I had ever done.

With less than two weeks to go, I contacted my friend Alex Merry, a public-speaking coach, for help. He got me to practise my TEDx talk, the one I had been honing for five months, in the middle of Hyde Park Corner in front of crowds of random people. Let's just say it didn't stop people in their tracks. Even worse, Alex looked bored. Then a thought occurred to me. As I was wrapping up, I said, 'I want to share something with you that I've been thinking about but haven't really had the courage to talk about. Let me know what you think.' And I shared my personal experience of what it was like to quit my job to start a business and how damn hard I had found it; how lonely I had been at times, and how I had wished more people opened up about it. I talked about why we need to stop this glorification of entrepreneurship, and about how the media seems to imply that becoming an entrepreneur is the only way to be truly happy – *spoiler alert*: it isn't!

Studies show that it's actually quite the opposite.

According to research by Dr Michael Freeman, who co-authored the 2015 report 'Are Entrepreneurs Touched with Fire?' – one of the only studies on the link between entrepreneurs and mental health – entrepreneurs are 50 per cent more likely to report having a mental health condition. In fact, Freeman found that entrepreneurs are twice as likely to suffer from depression, three times more likely to suffer from substance abuse, and twice as likely to have suicidal thoughts.

I know, right? Quite the catch.

The moment I stopped talking and saw Alex's face, I knew it. He was no longer bored. He was smiling.

'That's the talk you need to give, dude.'

I had less than ten days to ditch my old talk and start a new one. Do I take the easy way out, stick to what I know and potentially deliver an average talk? Or do I do what I know is right in my heart, face my biggest fears head on, and start again from scratch?

As you probably know, I went for the latter. I decided that I'd rather fail at something that was real than get by with something that wasn't.

My partner Julie was pregnant at the time with our first child. I didn't want to one day have to look at my daughter and tell her I was too scared to do what I knew was right. That I ran away from the courageous thing I knew deep down I needed to do. That I chose the easy way out. That I'm sorry not to be a better role model.

Today, that TEDx talk has been viewed more than a million times. If I had stuck to the boring non-personal TEDx talk I had first prepared, I wouldn't have received a fraction of that.

# Why My TEDx Talk Hit a Million Views

The reason my TEDx talk has resonated with so many people is because, in sharing my personal story and experience, I created a universal experience for all those who recognise themselves in what I shared.

I shared my real experience of what it was like to start a business and why I thought so many people were drawn to starting a business in the first place. I addressed the reality of being an entrepreneur and how the lived experience of starting and growing a company from scratch was very different from what I felt was being portrayed in the press and on social media. Frankly, I was tired of people like me suffering in silence, so I bit the bullet and decided that if I was going to die on the sword of TEDx, I might as well do it swinging for something I believed in.

I dug deep and shared things that I was ashamed of and felt guilty about. I had bought into the *fake it until you make it* mantra and I never wanted people to know that I was struggling. The problem is, when you feel as though you never made it and have no idea how you ever will make it, then what? You're left with shame and a deep feeling of inadequacy. At least that's how I felt. But I summoned the courage to be authentic, to be myself in public, and to share not just my successes but also my failures and imperfections. I knew someone out there needed to hear what I had to say so they wouldn't feel alone, so they wouldn't feel stupid, wrong or inadequate.

The result? My TEDx talk, 'What They Don't Tell You about Entrepreneurship', became the most watched TEDx-Cardiff video to date.

I still get messages on social media, LinkedIn and emails from people telling me how grateful they are that I shared my experience, because it was their experience too.

## 'No One Will Give You a Job if They Know You're Depressed'

The struggle to tell your story honestly is real.

Opening myself up for my TEDx talk did not come easily. Like so many others, I've had moments when I was told, with good intentions, that opening up about my experience, or being me, might result in serious negative consequences, and I should therefore keep the truth to myself.

For me, one of those moments was with my mum. In 2009, I found myself back home after breaking up with my girlfriend and having quit my job. I moved from a home halfway around the world to my childhood bedroom. I felt as though I had taken a massive step back in my life. Here I was, in my parents' house, and, instead of being grateful, I bathed myself in shame and self-blame.

In short, I wasn't in a good place.

I was about to tell my mum that I thought maybe I was going through some mild depression when she said, 'Don't tell anyone! Not even Denis ...'

Denis is my best friend. Our mums met at the local market in Fontainebleau when they were pregnant with us. Denis has been stuck with me ever since.

'Why shouldn't I tell Denis?' I asked.

'Because no one will give you a job if they know you're depressed,' she replied.

And just like that, it was anchored in my mind that if people knew I was going through tough times and potentially suffering from depression, it could make me unemployable.

It's not my mum's fault. I mean, I get it. The stigma around mental health, although it is a million miles better today than it was back then, is still pretty heavy. Yet the irony is that being able to talk about the tough times I went through is the very reason my talk engaged so many people and went viral.

What we all crave deep down is connection on a human level, and nothing is more human than owning up to the fact that we are imperfect. That we mess up. In acknowledging our imperfections and speaking about the moments when we fell short we allow others to feel seen, heard and understood on this messy journey called 'life'.

But I also understand that it can be hard to face the idea of being truly seen in public, especially if we feel that the only way to make it through life and our business is to fly under the radar, and make sure we play small so as not to be called out or found out.

# My First Professional Talk

As our front-of-the-room trainer waved his mighty computer clicker, enthusiastically telling us what a difference we were about to make in the world, I couldn't help but think of what I would say to Richard Branson if he walked in right now.

This wasn't just some random daydream fantasy. I was sitting through our induction training day to become a Virgin StartUp mentor. And it just so happened that this was being carried out at their London HQ (which sort of looks like a spaceship).

The session kicked off by showing a slide with a picture of the main man himself, Sir Rich, casually sipping a cup of tea in the back of the very same room we were sitting in, telling us that 'it could happen, he sometimes pops in, you never know ...'.

Before I was able to launch myself fully into another fantasy of how Richard and I would become BFFs, and how he'd casually invite me to hang out on his private island to try out his zip line and play a few rounds of tennis, I was sent, along with the other budding Virgin StartUp mentors, to our first ice-breaking exercise. I was paired with Victoria, a professional woman of similar age who appeared to be rocking a Russian accent. I was right. She was Russian.

After hearing a bit about my story, of how I ended up in London and how I had recently written a book called *It's Not You, It's Me* (a *modus operandi* for unfulfilled professionals wanting to find more meaningful, fulfilling and entrepreneurial work), she shouted, 'Oh my God, you need to go and speak to my company! They're always looking for engaging speakers to motivate employees.'

By the time I got home, Victoria had already emailed her HR director, suggesting that they get in touch with me. I was shocked and amazed. I jumped on a call with the company's HR director and HR business partner to talk about how I could help them with engaging their employees at work.

After taking a moment to introduce ourselves, it became clear that one of the issues they faced as a company, like so many others, was the challenge of attracting, engaging and retaining top talent, especially the younger generation of employees, especially millennials and Gen Z. Employee turnover was costing them a ton of money and they needed help in fixing that problem. They really believed they had created a great place to work and that a lot of first-time employees didn't realise it. The HR director said, 'We'd love for you to come in and talk about how our employees can find more meaning in their work.'

'But you do know that I wrote a book about how to quit your job and do work you love, right?'

'Exactly, which is why we think they'll listen to you because you speak a similar language and can relate to their problem.'

I'm still amazed to this day that they had the courage and vision to bring me in.

I prepared like crazy because this was my first real paid corporate talk. I thought I did a really good job, but I could see that I wasn't lighting the fire in my audience as much I had hoped I would.

Arms were crossed, faces seemed hostile, and I wasn't sure if half the room still had a pulse. It's always nerve-racking to see such behaviour in the middle of making a point. I was trying to focus on my next slide, not my internal dialogue screaming, 'Dude, I think you're bombing here!'

However, at the end of my talk I opened up the floor for questions. That's when something shifted. People asked personal questions about my experience, asking me how I felt when I went through X or Y and then as a result of me opening up, they started sharing some of their own professional struggles too.

I could have answered questions and listened to their challenges for hours, but it was time to wrap up. As I quietly packed up my laptop, put my clicker away and made my way back to the elevator, my HR contact caught up with me.

Naturally, I took the opportunity to ask, 'So, was that okay? What did you think?'

'Overall I think it went okay and the people seemed to enjoy it. But I think it would have been amazing if you had shared more about you, if you had shared more about your story.'

I was stunned.

They wanted to hear *my story*? Why would anyone care about my story?

And I certainly didn't see how sharing my story was relevant to making my point that everyone deserves to be seen, heard and supported. I know, the irony ...

And yet here I was, feeling a little embarrassed that I had been given this opportunity but that I'd fallen short of having the impact I wanted simply because I hadn't had the courage or insight to share my story.

As it turned out, the reason they'd hired me was because I had shared my story during our introductory call. She knew that my story involved some uncomfortable truths, some real moments that we all go through. And felt her team could relate to that.

For years, I was bullied on a daily basis by my French schoolteachers because of my inability to spell, do maths or read out loud. I was shamed in front of my peers and made to believe that I wasn't worth anything because of it. And sadly, I began to believe that I deserved it.

As a result, I was held back a year, continued to struggle, and was eventually expelled, labelled as incompetent and lazy.

Being kicked out of school meant I had to look for a new one, but the school I wanted to go to wouldn't accept me because I had dreadlocks (I know, quite a sight, right?).

Instead, I ended up settling for a school that would have me, where some of my classmates were drug dealers and others robbed houses.

Of course, the chip on my shoulder that I've carried with me since I was six years old enabled me to push through and prove everyone wrong. I finished with the top mark in my year before heading off to a good university in the UK and getting a 2:1 with honours, the best result my family has ever had. I told this story on the phone and this was what had inspired the company to hire me.

# You Have to Own It

When Sonia, who had two decades of experience in her field, came to me for help to become an in-demand speaker and thought leader, I immediately took a liking to her energy and ability to light up a room, even on Zoom. Her smile was contagious and her enthusiasm bottomless. But like so many entrepreneurs and business leaders who come to see me, while she was really good at what she did, her clients loved working with her, and she managed to find some level of success, she felt that something was holding her back.

The problem was that most people didn't know the real her.

She too wanted to figure out how to get over the fears and mental barriers that prevented her from sharing more of herself and her true story in public, to better connect and engage with her ideal audience and her team.

Here's what she told me about what she was going through before she met me: 'People buy from people and I didn't feel like they really knew me, the person behind the brand. Being a different person at work and a different person at home, I felt like there were two people in the mirror. And I couldn't bring them together ...'

Like so many others, what Sonia really wanted wasn't just a five-step process on How to Tell Your Personal Story on a Big Stage. What she wanted was the courage to be vulnerable (and visible) in public, and the permission to be imperfect in a business context.

And I'm glad to report that she found just that by sharing her story more openly in various professional settings, from one-to-one calls with prospective clients to speaking on stages.

# Own It, Love It, Share It

If there's one thing I've learned, it's that most people think that learning how to share their personal story authentically in public is mostly about structure and communication, that it basically comes down to a marketing and communications issue.

But the truth is, marketing, communications and other practical issues are less than 10 per cent of the problem. The other 90 per cent is in your head: you, your story, and *owning all of it*, the good and the bad, the pretty and the ugly. Not just the convenient or professional bits, not just the fun and pleasant bits, not just the bits you're proud of. No, you have to own the whole lot. Whether you share the whole lot is a different story. What I'm talking about is the ability to face your biggest fears and acknowledge that, like everyone else, your story holds moments that are emotionally charged, that you'd rather forget, wish had never happened or hope no one ever finds out about.

And yet, more often than not, it is those very darkest moments that have shaped who we are, for better or worse. Those moments are what make us human and what attract people the most. And seeing the humanity in ourselves and in others, acknowledging that life is full of messy bits and pieces, allows us to better connect to ourselves and, in turn, to others.

That's why I wholeheartedly believe in the transformative power of learning how to unpack, own and share your story in public. You see, it's not just about the business benefits that you will experience from embracing this process, of which you will have plenty; it's the ability for you to drop your shoulders, for you to talk a little louder, to hold your head a bit higher, to feel a little less tense, a little less afraid of what others might think. It's the ability to walk into a room without any fear of what people might or might not know about you; the knowledge that nothing anyone could say could damage your reputation because there's nothing you're not willing to own. Because you're comfortable in your own skin.

It's the ability to walk on any stage, at any time, at any place; to jump on any medium or platform, knowing that you ultimately have nothing to hide, because you no longer need to be one person in public and another in private. It's the ultimate freedom. It means having no fear of what people might think of you. It means no longer walking around afraid of being found out. On the contrary, you can't wait to share your story because you know it will act as an effortless and natural magnet for your ideal audience.

## The Authenticity Gap

What does it take to be more comfortable being yourself in public?

There's no short answer of course, but here's a start. Narrow the gap between who you say you are and who you actually are, and narrow the gap between what you say you do and what you actually do. In short, narrow the gap between who you think you should be and who you really are.

I call this space the Authenticity Gap.

And my theory is that the smaller that gap is, the more you get to enjoy business and life. And the more people trust you and your word.

It takes time and work to close the gap between who we think we ought to be and accept who we really are, but trust me, it's worth the journey.

# Giving Yourself Permission to Be Imperfect in Public Makes You More Influential

I think we all want to be at peace with who we are and want to give ourselves permission to let the world see and experience us as we really are. It takes a lot less energy to be yourself than it does to try to pretend to be someone else, or to hide in the shadows hoping no one will find you.

There's a reason why most criminals on the run finally end up getting caught or turning themselves in, as it's a tough and lonely life constantly living in the shadows.

I used to dread the thought of anyone knowing that I was dyslexic or that I was held back a year at school and eventually kicked out of the conventional education system when I was sixteen. But today I'm able to share that information with anyone and anywhere, without feeling an ounce of shame or guilt. It's the freedom that comes with owning the parts of me that I thought should be hidden or kept a secret.

It's the power of healing your wounds and sharing your scars. Freeing up the energy, attention and time you currently spend on holding back, trying to remain in control of any potential outcome, pretending to be someone you're not will allow you to make so much more mental space for the things that actually matter.

That's the power of giving yourself the permission to be your effortless self and unlocking your story. That's why I'm so passionate about doing this work, because I know the ripple effect it can have on your life, your business and your audience.

I know the ripple effect it can have on your relationships with your friends, colleagues, clients, kids, partner and, more importantly, with yourself.

It's time for you to come home to who you truly are and own the impact your story can have. It's time to start putting the pieces in place that will allow you to take this momentous step into the next chapter of your life.

It's time to turn the page in this book and in your private and public personas.

*It's time to get real.*

# CHAPTER THREE

# People Buy from People

*We live in an attention economy. People now have limitless options available to them, with limited time in which to consume them.*

Toby Wiseman, Editor in Chief,
*Men's Health* magazine[6]

We hear the word all the time. *Profile*. And if you're in business, you know you need to raise it because you hear about it everywhere you go: 'You need to raise your profile!'

In short, your profile is what people say about you when you're not in the room. It's your reputation. It's what comes up on search engines when people look you up; it's what people say when someone asks about you. Your profile is also why you come up in conversations even when you're not around.

It's the information you put out into the world and what others put out about you.

It's the picture, feeling and flavour people get of you before they even meet you.

You've guessed it, your profile is your personal brand.

Now I want to make a clear distinction. Your profile is separate and different from the branding of your business or the branding of your products or services. Even though they can absolutely be interlinked, you must treat your profile at first as something independent that eventually becomes fuel for any of your ventures.

As you will learn, no matter what business you've started, there's a big fat chance that you started it because you cared about the problem you were solving and the people you were trying to help, most likely because something you personally experienced led you to want to fix it.

Your business brand is the DNA of your company, it's what you project to the world in terms of values, value proposition, positioning and marketing. It can be a powerful emotional connection too, don't get me wrong, but according to an article in *Entrepreneur*, 'consumers connect more strongly with a personality than with a faceless brand'.[7] In other words, people don't relate to a faceless brand the same way they relate to the person behind it.

In case it's helpful, let me make another distinction. Your product or service brand is the promise you make to the world about what your product or service aims to solve (e.g. the famous 23 October Steve Jobs keynote at Apple Music Event 2001 where he launched the iPod with 'a thousand songs in your pocket').[8] It's how people recognise your product or service as a solution to their problem.

Your profile, on the other hand, is who you are and what you stand for. It's your take on your industry, it's the causes you support, it's the ventures you believe in. It's you sharing your story and standing up for something you believe in. It's about your values, your vision and the origin story of how you came to be and why you do what you do.

If you're here then I know you understand the importance of putting yourself out there, but chances are you're deeply uncomfortable at the idea of doing it or know that you're holding back from truly showing up when you do it.

That's because you're not yet embracing your super-power ...

# Your Story Is the Secret Hack You've Been Waiting For

Beyond the need to raise your profile, building trust, connection and relatability with your audience and your team are also key to succeeding in business and having the impact you want. Problem is, these days, it can sometimes feel as though what you need to stand out from the crowd in a noisy digital world are million-dollar marketing budgets.

It turns out, what gets people to pay attention and want to do business with you isn't so much the amount you spend on your marketing budget but rather how much you care; that is, how you position yourself and your business as the emotional glue.

Your story accelerates this process. It's how people get people to know you, like you and trust you. That's right, as we've already covered, one of the fastest ways to create a connection with your audience is to allow them to hear you share your story authentically. Your story is the only thing truly unique about you and it can act as a magnet to your ideal customers or as a repellent to your time-wasters, such as those who clearly have no intention to work with you but still like to take up all of your time.

And nothing conveys a message or an idea better than a powerful story well told.

# When It Comes to Connecting with People, Storytelling Is Your BFF

We are emotionally wired to connect with other people around stories and messages. It's how we make sense of the world around us.

Stories are our native tongue, so you'd be crazy not to learn the language that works best when it comes to connecting and engaging with people to get them to care about what you have to say and offer. After all, we connect with people and faces more than we connect with pretty much anything else in the world. When you are able to put a face to your brand by sharing your story, you are able to contextualise a product or service in a familiar narrative that feels safe, engaging and trustworthy. When we do this well, our stories gain the quality of *narrative transportation*; they compel our audience to become fully immersed in our stories.

When James Routledge, author of *Mental Health at Work* and founder of Sanctus – a London-based organisation tackling the taboos linked to mental health in the workplace – first shared the story behind Sanctus, he started with his *personal story*. Every meeting, every introduction kicked off with James explaining why he was so passionate about changing the conversation around mental health at work.

In his 2016 Medium post 'Mental Health in Startups', James shared publicly for the first time that he was struggling with his mental health in the wake of shutting down his first business: 'in the last year I've struggled with stress, anxiety, panic attacks and sleepless nights'.[9]

After working for a venture capital firm and being on the other side of the table, hearing entrepreneurs desperately trying to pitch their ventures for funding, clearly struggling behind the scenes, he realised that he wasn't the only founder struggling in silence. That's why he wanted to break the taboo around mental health in start-ups and share his experience too.

The reaction to his article was overwhelming: 200-plus personal emails from people in start-ups thanking him for opening up, 13,000 reads of the original blog post and non-stop notifications.[10]

Shortly after, *The Guardian* got in touch and asked James to write an article.

'From rags to riches, how a university drop-out launched a tech start-up, raised $1 million whilst building a product used by 130 websites reaching 50m users every month and lived the dream ...' So could have run the pull-out blurb for James's story, if it weren't for the fact that he decided to burst the BS bubble and shine a light on an experience that so many others can relate to.

Instead, he titled his article '"Sleep Faster" Start-up Culture Puts Entrepreneurs' Mental Health at Risk'.

Listening to James's story, and his journey to open up about his mental health, you can't help but be moved by and engaged with the mission behind his organisation, because you know he isn't doing it because it's the cool thing to do, or because he's after a quick buck. It just adds up in your brain that you can trust this person to care enough about the problem they're solving because they, in turn, can relate and empathise with what their audience, customers or clients are going through.

That's why I want to help you unpack, shape and share your story.

Because the reality is, no matter how great your product or service is, no matter how good you are at what you do, no matter what results you get for your clients, if the world doesn't know about you and how much you care and why they should care too, then you will always fall short of your full potential.

Think about it. Why do the most pioneering companies and forward-thinking brands attract the world's top talent and build bases of raving fans around the world?

It's often because the founders of those organisations came out of the shadows and publicly shared their stories, enrolling people through their message and their vision, and explaining why they do what they do.

Stories provide clarity. They help us understand how to process our feelings, our emotions and our thoughts, and help us make sense of the world around us.

We all want to be part of an exciting story.

As Bobette Buster, author of *Do Story: How to Tell Your Story So the World Listens* (2013), once said, 'stories also have the power to heal, to share a vision and most of all, to inspire others'.

Stories literally have the ability to change the way we think or act.

And if that isn't a superpower, I don't know what is.

That's why the success of your business is heavily based on how well you tell your story and how much you're willing to step outside of the shadows, because today's world wants to know you and the real story behind why you do what you do.

If you're in business, and you have an important mission or message to share, then it's vital you learn to tell your story well.

# Harsh Reality

The hard truth is, if all things are equal, customers will always pick the brand or company whose founder's story they can identify with, who supports a cause bigger than just financial gains, and whose leaders they feel they know, like and trust.

Dr J. J. Peterson, co-author of *Marketing Made Simple* (2020), puts it this way: 'The best products don't always win in the marketplace. The products and brands that communicate the clearest are the ones who win. Whoever tells a better story, wins.'

It explains why the likes of accomplished CEOs Jessica Alba, Richard Branson, Oprah Winfrey, Tim Cook or Elon Musk have a much larger following than any of their respective companies do. It's because the stories behind how they ended up doing what they do and why they became who they are are what move us and touch us on a deeper level. They're people like you and me who have found a way to find the missing piece in the puzzle that is their enigma, namely how to get out of their own way to put themselves out there and tell their story and impact the world with their message.

# The Cost Is Courage

If information was all you needed then you could put this book down and go try your best to put yourself out there and share your story with the world. Problem is, life doesn't really work like that, does it?

When it comes to raising your profile, the obstacle for almost everybody is how to share our stories publicly. Becoming more known, liked and trusted isn't informational, it's emotional.

There are hundreds of thousands of articles online on how to leverage social media, get featured in the press or speak publicly to raise your profile, as well as articles on how to structure your story or talk like those of some of history's greatest orators.

But the truth is, unless you deal with the emotional journey of putting yourself out there by sharing your story and raising your profile, you will always struggle to achieve what you set out to achieve.

## Ask Me How I Know ...

It took me ten years of trying to start and grow a business, six years of trying harder and four years of therapy to realise that unless I addressed the core reason of why I was self-sabotaging, procrastinating, holding back, jumping from one idea to the next, without finishing anything, I would forever be stuck searching for the miracle cure.

There is no external miracle cure. The miracle we are all looking for is within us. The only problem is that it comes at a cost. And that cost is courage.

When my client Ash shared his story with me, something didn't add up.

Sure, as a former specialist military unit colonel in the British Armed Forces, world championship athlete, international award-winning musician and someone decorated a number of times by Her Majesty the Queen, he had achieved some pretty extraordinary things in his life.

But despite all these accolades and epic achievements, something was missing. And I couldn't quite put my finger on it.

Until, that is, we sat down to unpack his story and started talking about his early childhood.

It turns out that Ash grew up in a pretty traumatic environment with an abusive, alcoholic father. And Ash often had to put himself in front of his mother and sisters to protect them from his father.

That's when it clicked. No wonder Ash was so driven to take care of his team, be it colleagues at work or soldiers on the battlefield. It suddenly made sense why he focused his time and energy on helping companies create better cultures or, in his daughter's words, 'help people play nicely at work'.

When I asked Ash if he had ever shared the story about his father, he said, 'Of course not, why would I?'

My job is never to push anyone but simply to highlight a story that they haven't yet fully owned that could be key to connecting with their audience the way they, deep down, need to. Like all things in life, sometimes it's not ready until it's ready.

Around a year later, I heard back from Ash. He told me he had been thinking deeply about what we discussed and he was, finally, ready to share his full story. He opened up for the first time during an interview on a podcast, which both moved me and filled me with such a sense of pride. Not because I was proud of my work and the small part I had played, but because I knew that when Ash owned his story it would do more than help him grow his business and connect on a human and authentic level with more people. His words freed him from the trauma he had experienced in his childhood and helped him move beyond his fears, by accepting that there can be immense strength in vulnerability. And his story could have a tremendous impact on others who need to hear it.

As a result, Ash felt a new sense of freedom, as if he had got rid of the shackles holding him back from truly connecting and engaging with his audience. His keynote speeches became more powerful and his content even more magnetic.

By sharing some of his childhood experiences as well as the intense trauma and loss of leading men and women in combat, Ash became more human and relatable in the eyes and ears of his audience. He was no longer a superhero, a decorated military leader or an athlete who had achieved so many things and overcome so many obstacles. Instead, he was like us – human – someone who hurts and someone who has found a way to turn his pain into his purpose.

In fact, I would argue that the record-breaking popularity of Daniel Craig as James Bond is owing to the complexity and humanity of Craig's version of the character. It allows us to see a more vulnerable and human side of Bond.

## Welcome to the World's Biggest Club

I'm convinced that that *connection*, that power of storytelling to make others feel less alone, is why my TEDx talk reached over a million views and has connected with entrepreneurs, freelancers, founders, coaches, consultants, speakers, solopreneurs and business leaders around the world.

And that's why, despite all the internal alarm bells and defence mechanisms that tried to short-circuit my intentions, I spoke about my real experience of dealing with self-doubt, fears and insecurities on the yo-yo emotional journey of starting a business.

The original title of my talk was 'The Dark Side of Entrepreneurship', because on that day, on that stage, I said out loud what the vast majority of people who are crazy enough to think they can make a living by making a difference, experience every single day. But they often suffer in silence, stuck in quiet desperation. Opening up and sharing my experience was a huge relief. It was like an enormous weight had been lifted from my shoulders and I was finally free. Not only that, my business didn't suffer. Quite the contrary. And my talk enabled others to feel as though they weren't the only ones who experience those difficult moments.

It enabled me to have more empathy with CEOs and founders who, in turn, felt safe opening up to me so we could get to the real core of what was holding them back from engaging and inspiring their people.

Behind the glamorous accounts of stories of founders going from zero to a billion dollars lies a reality that, for many of us, is too often ignored. The crippling fear of being judged or criticised for saying the wrong thing, or of coming across as incompetent or stupid. That's why, in my candid talk, I drew on my experience of what it's really like to quit your job to start your own business.

It took months for me to find the courage to pull the trigger on unleashing the real me in my talk. I dragged my feet for weeks, wishing there was a different way. I thought about all the different ways I could get out of having to give my TEDx talk. But I realised there was no other choice if I wanted to have the biggest impact I could. So I pushed through, even though I, too, felt like a total fraud; like I had blagged my way into getting invited to give a TEDx talk and it was only a matter of time before the organisers realised they had made a big fat mistake.

The irony is that by opening up about my experience I realised that so many other people experienced the same feelings.

So if you feel as though you could never be as inspiring or engaging as the people you see on stage, online, in the media or on a podcast, think again.

In fact, if you feel stuck on your journey to impact, it probably has nothing to do with your natural-born abilities. It's more likely because of the story you've made up over the years around your ability to be compelling (or not) and who you need to be or become in order to have the impact you want.

*That* is the story we need to rewrite and change so that you can start to experience what it's like to see your message turn into a movement.

# You Can Be in Denial or You Can Be in Charge, but You Can't Be Both

As a parent, the following statement shocked me when I first came across it. According to a 2010 study by internet security firm AVG, '92 percent of US children have some type of online presence by the time they are two years old'. And more than a third had digital lives before they were born.[11]

This means that, although we may not all have a choice over what is being said or posted about us when we grow up, most of us have a choice over what we decide the world gets to see, hear or know about us.

In fact, you have *two* choices. You either jump in the driver's seat and take control of the narrative of what the world, your potential partners, future employees and clients get to see, hear, watch and read about you; or you cross your fingers, let luck and the unknown take care of it, and hope for the best.

My guess is, if you managed to get to where you are today and have found some level of success in your business and life, it's because you believe in making things happen and taking responsibility for your actions. You believe in having a measure of control over your life.

It's time to control your story. It's time to get out of the shadows, remove your head from the ground and start looking at ways to feel excited about sharing your story, your message and the impact you want to have on the world.

Here's the good news. I'm here to tell you to ditch the advice you've heard about faking it until you make it. You do not need to become someone else in order to become more you.

Sure, for tribute bands it works a treat, and being inspired by someone else can be a great way to get started. But when it comes to being more compelling and engaging, nothing beats figuring out who you really are and letting the world know about it by giving yourself the permission to fail in public. I know it's helped me show up more powerfully, to remind myself that being imperfect in public gives permission to others to do the same.

You can engage and enrol your ideal audience without having to be someone you're not or act like someone you don't want to be. This isn't about becoming a cookie cutter version of yourself based on some other person's template you've seen or heard.

No. This is about being unapologetically yourself, owning your successes and failures, highs and lows, and accepting the fact that being yourself is good for business.

It requires a tremendous amount of courage, but if you're here, today, reading this book, I believe in my heart that you yearn to be called forth and to be given a road map on how to finally get your story and message out there.

This isn't about making it all about you, but rather about making it about the people you're trying to reach and ultimately serve. It's about having the courage to tell your life-changing story in a powerful and authentic way. In order to do that, we need to talk about the importance of mastering and fully adopting *storytelling* as part of your toolkit.

# CHAPTER FOUR

# The Power of the Story

If you want people to pay attention and care about what you have to say, nothing does the job better than a tool that's been around since the dawn of time.

## Stories Transport Us

Most people can remember where they were when a life-changing event happened. For example, if you were born before 1995, there's a good chance you can remember when the planes hit the World Trade Center, and that you can paint a detailed picture of where you were, how you found out, and what was going on. You can viscerally remember what you were doing at that very moment.

Others, like my mum, recall what it was like staring at a small screen watching the first man walk on the moon, on 20 July 1969.

Some remember finding out about the assassination of Martin Luther King Jr on 4 April 1968, or hearing that John Lennon had been shot in December 1980, or that Princess Diana had died in a car crash in August 1997.

These events and so many others can leave an everlasting impact that is somehow carved into our collective and individual memories.

For me, one of these life-changing events wasn't a historical defining moment as such, however. It was seeing my first film on the big screen. You see, a memorable, life-defining story doesn't *have* to be a worldwide dramatic event. It can be as simple as watching a movie.

It was 1988 and my dad took my brother and I to our local cinema, L'Ermitage, in Fontainebleau, France, to see *L'Ours* (*The Bear*), directed by Jean-Jacques Annaud. It was a pretty big deal because my big brother would usually go alone with my dad (as I was too young), while I stayed behind probably trying to see how many sponges I could fit in my mouth.

We collected our tickets and made our way to our seats. An usher showed us to our seats with a flashlight, while someone else stood in the aisle with a tray of delicious treats before the film started and during the interval (yes, there were intervals at the cinema when I was a kid!).

I climbed up and did my best to stand up straight on my foldable seat, which felt more like a sandwich with me in the middle.

I remember being mesmerised by the ads and trailers that came on before the picture started, and how my brother hogged all the popcorn. As the film began, I was transported to a beautiful mountainside where a mother bear and her cub were searching for food between wobbly rocks on a slippery slope.

They were cute, and you could tell that the mummy bear cared deeply for her baby bear. He even made a few funny noises that got me giggling.

But then I realised that what I thought was going to be a lovely film about how mummy bears and baby bears learn how to hunt and roll in the meadows, happily ever after, was actually something straight out of a horror movie ...

That's right, I might as well have been staring at Bambi, except it wasn't a cartoon, and instead of hearing a gunshot in the far distance, I actually saw the mama bear killed in a rockslide following an encounter with a beehive. We followed the cub's struggle to survive, desperately trying to befriend a male grizzly bear who couldn't care less, only to then be captured by hunters and find itself fighting for its life, narrowly escaping the clenching jaws of a committed cougar.

Needless to say, I was screaming my head off and crying, snot and all, shouting at the screen the entire time.

My dad asked me if I wanted to leave, but I didn't. I wanted to know what happened to the cub, if it would indeed survive and if the grizzly bear would stop being in such a pissy mood and actually show the cub some love. (Spoiler alert: it eventually does and actually saves the bear from the hungry cougar.)

What I learned that day, apart from realising that bees don't like it when you poke around in their honey, is that stories touch and connect with us in ways that no other medium can.

What I experienced that day, at the ripe old age of four, was *narrative transportation.*

Narrative transportation is the ability to invite someone into a story, or your story, in such a way that the person listening or watching is fully immersed in the experience, forgetting what is going on around them. And it just so happens that narrative transportation has the ability to change the way we feel.

That's why we love watching films, TV series or documentaries. It's why we love going to the cinema and why we spent over £5.64 billion in the film industry in the UK in 2021.[12] We love a good story because stories move us and enable us to experience something new or different, or escape our own reality, even if just for a short while.

If you want to influence, engage or inspire people then you need to learn how to connect to what matters: making them feel something. And that involves stories.

# Stories Influence How We Feel (and How We Act)

A clear, visceral experience of this realisation happened when I was three years old in nursery school. I was cast as a dragon for the annual nursery play. Of course, my ego took a little bruising at the idea of not being the knight in shining armour saving the damsel in distress, but I made sure to make the most of my role. I was supposed to be killed by the knight coming to save the princess, but instead of falling down quietly to my death I made sure to put on a proper performance and die a slow, over-the-top death in front of the audience.

That's the first time I remember hearing a collective laugh because of something I did.

I enjoyed it so much that I got back up and started running around again, to the great despair of both the boy playing the knight and the teacher who thought she had everything under control.

I was the chink in her armour.

There and then, as I repeatedly died and got up and made all the parents laugh, I knew there was something truly special about connecting with an audience when you focus on how you want to make them feel, too. Of course, the teacher eventually stepped in and told me to stay dead so she could drag me away by my feet. Even so, I didn't go without a cheeky wave and a grin to the crowd.

What's interesting is that that singular event, back when I was a three-year-old boy dressed up as a dragon, has defined so much of how I connect with an audience today. I always focus my attention on how I want my audience to feel. Sometimes I feel as though I'm losing the crowd, and the way I respond is to name it. It shifts the space. Plus, setting the intention of what energy I want to create in the space has served me well over the years, getting me closer to the desired impact I want my talks and keynotes to have.

Now if I'm going to stand here and tell you that your imperfections make you more influential and that sharing your mistakes is a superpower, I'm going to have to share the story I've been reluctant to share publicly until now ...

## Flowers for Africa

A few weeks before my twelfth birthday, I somehow managed to convince my best friend Denis, who had just returned from a few years in the US, to come with me and snatch flowers from my parents' garden to sell door to door to make a bit of money to buy sweets at the bakery down the road.

Now I will say this. I'm not proud of what I'm about to share, but if the truth sets you free then freedom here I come.

Denis wasn't too sure about this scheme, like he wasn't about most of the adventures in which I ensnared him, be it jumping from a tree or pouring petrol down a new-found well and setting light to it, blowing us up in the air (true story).

But as always, he was kind enough to let me convince him, and willing to give it a go. For legal purposes, let me make it clear that this was, of course, my idea, and Denis probably had no choice since I was really good at emotionally blackmailing him. After all, he had moved to Florida, so in my eyes he owed me this much, having taken off and left his best friend behind.

Armed with our newly collected lilies, innocent angelic smiles, my questionable morals and lack of inhibition when talking to random strangers, while rocking a haircut only a medieval monk could be proud of, we started making our way down the street.

There was only one problem. No one was interested in sponsoring two eleven-year-olds' sweet-shopping sprees.

So I came up with an idea: what if we said it was all for charity? *Charity* was the missing piece of our candy-gorging dreams. We would raise money for children in Africa! I had bought my one-way ticket to hell.

Now we had a story and a business model, unethical and questionable to be sure, but I really believed they would work.

'Dude, this is so wrong on so many levels,' Denis grumbled.

'I know, but do you have a better idea?'

No. Denis did not.

We approached the first door, and I gave it a firm knock, not once but three times. I mean, if you're going to go to hell and bullshit your way to make your cavity-filled dreams come true, you might as well do it with intent.

I took a step back, pushed my hair away from my forehead, pulled my trousers up, and got ready to launch into an improvised speech with a million-dollar smile only an angelic car salesman could pull off.

Knowing Denis, he was probably hiding in a bush behind me, red as a tomato, hoping I'd get caught.

'Hi, we're selling fresh flowers today to collect money for children in Africa and we were wondering if you'd be interested in taking part in helping our cause?'

To my surprise, the woman at the door smiled and said, 'Oh, how great! Wait, give me a minute so I can get my purse.' It wasn't a joke, she really did run up the stairs to fetch her purse.

I couldn't believe it. My heart raced like crazy. My plan had worked.

Yes, I would most likely pay a heavy cosmic price for it, but damn, I might as well be up for an Oscar for Most Compelling Bullshit Fundraiser. If only the Oscars were a celebration of the world's worst people.

As I stood there waiting to receive what felt like a small fortune, I thought about all the other doors we still had to go knocking on and wished I'd thought of this idea a lot sooner.

The woman at the door handed over a few francs in exchange for a few flowers, freshly snatched from our garden (which my parents obviously didn't know about). I thanked her with a smile and off we went to the next house.

Let's just say we made a killing that day, and not just of our souls. We had never seen so much money in our lives.

Did we have a change of heart and hand the money back to everyone? Did we pull a 180 and hand the cash to our parents so they could make a charitable donation?

No. Of course not.

We marched straight to the local bakery, dropped our bag of coins on the counter as if we were buying the place, and asked the confused woman behind the till to fill the biggest bag she had with the most delicious treats, making sure we pointed out the good ones, of course.

I had never seen such a big bag of sweets in my life. We could barely carry it!

We did our best to hoover down as many as possible on our way home and I'm pretty sure we hid the rest somewhere as our parents would clearly have been suspicious of how we had come across such a tasty fortune.

The sweet taste of candy sugar-coated whatever guilt and shame we may have felt, at least for a while. The irony is that Denis had a dental appointment a few days later. He had four cavities.

Needless to say, I feel conflicted about sharing this story.

On one hand, I'm weirdly impressed and proud of the young Mark, who took on the entrepreneurial pursuit of generating income both for himself and his best friend to enjoy their favourite sweets by making the most of what he had (flowers, stories and neighbours).

On the other hand, I'm deeply ashamed of the highly unethical behaviour I displayed and regret having used a fabrication to con people into giving me their hard-earned money for starving children on the African continent.

But what I learned that day is that stories are the most powerful way to influence behaviour. We can use stories for good or for bad.

Stories are also an opportunity for us to be authentic (or not). My inauthenticity that day probably bought me a one-way ticket to hell, something I can never take back but only learn from.

That's why I promised myself, after confessing to my parents and being reminded of how wrong it is to lie to people and to profit from the suffering of others, that I would never repeat the same mistakes and that I would only use stories for good.

# We Are Hard-wired for Stories

Jennifer Aaker, a marketing professor at Stanford Graduate School of Business, says that 'our brains are wired to understand and retain stories'.[13]

According to Carmine Gallo's 2016 book *The Storyteller's Secret*, some 200,000 years ago, when we first discovered fire and started cooking food, our brains went through a developmental leap. Our larynxes lengthened and in turn we could speak more clearly, verbalising our thoughts and communicating our needs. Gathered around the fire at night, our ancestors would eat, connect and share stories.

Anthropologists believe that we spent up to 80 per cent of our time back then sharing stories to help each other learn how to hunt, avoid predators and find food and shelter. As a result, great storytellers were most likely great tribal leaders too.

That's why storytelling became important. It enables us to share and pass on information in a way that is memorable, helpful and pivotal to our survival. If you didn't pay attention or listen carefully enough to stories then you might not survive. You wouldn't learn from the mistakes of others, learn how to find the nutrients you needed to survive, learn how to find shelter or a mate to reproduce with.

Throughout history, as a species, we have tried to make sense of the world through stories, be it prehistoric people's depictions of mammoth hunting found in the caves of Lascaux, or those of Egyptians, who found a way to capture their beliefs and stories using hieroglyphs.

No matter how you look at it, we've always found a way to capture our imagination, share our experiences and translate our thoughts through stories.

Someone who had a deep understanding of this concept was Joseph Campbell, an American professor of comparative mythology and comparative religion, who studied the religion and stories and mythologies of different cultures across the world. What he discovered was that although we may think we hold different and unique stories depending on where and when we were born, in reality all foundational stories are structured around the exact same framework. Campbell called it the 'monomyth' or 'the hero's journey', which he explored in his 1949 doorstopper of a book, *The Hero with a Thousand Faces*.

Whether you've heard of Joseph Campbell and his hero's journey or not, chances are you most definitely have been on the receiving end of his work and impact. George Lucas credits Campbell's work as a major inspiration for

*Star Wars*, among countless other Hollywood films and franchises. From *The Matrix* to the *Harry Potter* saga, from *Finding Nemo* to *The Wizard of Oz*, all films and novels follow the same structure as Joseph Campbell's monomyth.

So what *is* the hero's journey? It's the theory that in order for a story to be compelling, it must contain a few crucial elements. Just as for a song to sound good and be in tune, so a story needs to hit a series of notes in a particular sequence. It needs a protagonist, i.e. a character, who goes from being in an ordinary world to suddenly facing a challenge and being called to go on an adventure. At this point, the hero (or heroine) will at first refuse the call to adventure, only to eventually accept the quest, be forced to learn hard and difficult lessons along the way, meet allies and face foes and enemies, to eventually face their innermost fear, vanquish their biggest challenge, and become a transformed version of themselves so they may return to their world changed and able to give back, only to repeat the sequence all over again, but from a new place that reflects growth and change.

Joseph Campbell's work demonstrated that stories exist across all religions and cultures, because stories are the best and most effective way to convey ideas, messages, philosophies, lessons, morals and values to others.

We all seek and crave a narrative that helps us make sense of our world. That's why we will always choose the most compelling story available. That's why your customers are begging you to share a clear and engaging story.

# The Stories We Like to Hear

Good public-relations campaigns are all about storytelling, and any good PR specialist will tell you that people respond to seven primary story types.

- **Redemption**: I messed up but I've mended my ways. I've hurt people, but I've changed and now I'm making up for my past errors. I used to be a crook, a drug addict, an alcohol abuser, a drug dealer, but now I've changed. Redemption happens through bringing compassion and connection to the hurt version of ourselves, not just stopping the behaviour.

- **Resurrection**: I was down and out, now I'm successful. My company went bankrupt, now it's hugely successful. I used to mop floors for a living, now I'm the CEO. The failure I experienced gave me exactly the right tools to prevail.

- **Reinvention**: I used to be mean and cynical but now I'm an optimistic humanitarian. I used to sell my soul for money, now I'm having a positive impact. I used to work in a toxic industry, but I retrained myself and succeeded on the cutting edge of the new circular economy.

- **Self-reflection**: I experienced a spiritual awakening. My purpose in life isn't what I thought it was. I've grown to treasure people and experiences more than money and objects.

- **Survival**: I overcame the odds. I was married to an abusive spouse, but I freed myself and haven't let the experience sour my outlook. I was severely injured on the battlefield but I overcame my limitations and learned to thrive in spite of them. A cancer diagnosis nearly crushed me, but I picked myself up and soldiered on in the face of terrible odds.

- **Love**: I used to believe I wasn't worthy of love, but now I help others fall in love with who they really are. My life was transformed when I discovered my soulmate. I was lost and without purpose until I found my passion. I was down and depressed, but finding my purpose showed me the beauty of life.

- **Freedom**: I was stifled by an oppressive corporate culture so I left and started my own company. I grew up in a rigid, controlling home so my own home is filled with acceptance and spontaneity.

As you think about your own past, ask yourself how the episodes of your history fit into the above story types. If they do, you're already well on your way to an engaging story.

In Part Two of this book you will be able to leverage that knowledge into creating a more compelling story by learning and applying a simple yet practical framework.

# Stories Connect Us

Uri Hasson, a neuroscientist at Princeton University, studies how we tell and hear stories – and how a great story may even allow two brains to sync up. According to Dr Hasson, functional magnetic resonance imaging (fMRI) experiments show that at the start, the brainwave activities of a story-teller and a listener are different – as you'd expect them to be. But as the storyteller starts sharing their story the MRI picks up interesting activity: the brainwaves of the listener match the brainwaves of the storyteller.[14]

When we hear stories, our amygdala, an almond-shaped cluster of nuclei deep in our brain's cerebrum, activates and dictates our emotions and behaviour, meaning that stories can literally impact and influence the way we feel and act.

As a species we can tap into each other's psyches through stories and relate to each other's emotions. That's how powerful stories can be. They allow you to speak to the primal decision-making system of other people by tapping into their feelings.

If you want to connect to someone's heart, you must first connect to their brain by telling a clear and powerful story.

## Stories Sell

One of my favourite studies conducted around the power of storytelling was Significant Objects, a literary and anthropological experiment devised by Rob Walker and Joshua Glenn in 2009.[15] What Walker and Glenn found was that narratives make insignificant objects significant. They realised that stories are the Trojan horse to influencing our behaviour, be it what we think, feel or do.

The experiment curators purchased objects for no more than a few dollars from thrift stores and garage sales. Then they assigned a writer to each object tasked with writing a fictional story, in any style or voice, about the object. And each significant object would be listed for sale on eBay.

The winning bidder would be mailed the significant object along with a printout of the object's fictional story. Net proceeds from the sales were given to the respective authors and I believe they gave a portion back to charity, too.

The question we all have is, did it work? Are people willing to pay more than expected based on an emotional connection being created through sharing a story about the object?

To give you some context, they spent around $129 in total on the items, averaging $1.25 apiece. They generated a whopping $8,000 in sales. That's a 6,000 per cent growth by simply adding a story to each object.

**What they discovered is that the more emotionally invested we are, the less critical we become.**

Stories have a direct impact on how we feel and how we act. That's why embracing your story as part of getting people to pay attention and care about what you have to say or share is so important.

Think about it. Why are so many people willing to queue for hours or days to buy products, be it the latest mobile phone or the pair of limited edition trainers? And why are we willing to spend huge amounts of money on branded products that are available in far less expensive versions from other companies?

It's because of the story we've been told and how we've connected to it. It's how we feel being part of that story. We stop making rational decisions. Because emotion and connection are how stories sell products, and it just so happens that sharing our personal stories can act as an emotional and connection glue for our audience.

That's why, if you genuinely have an interest in helping people care about what you have to say, share or sell, if you want people to rave about your brand, product or service, then you simply cannot afford to ignore the power of storytelling.

I know what you're thinking, though. Yes, you get the power of storytelling and you can see how brands and individuals have been using story to leverage influence, income and impact, but how is all this relevant to you and your particular audience or situation?

*I'm so glad you asked.*

# CHAPTER FIVE

# The Benefits of Sharing Your Story

*I tell my story not because it is unique, but because it is the story of so many girls.*

Malala Yousafzai, Pakistani activist for female education and a Nobel Peace Prize laureate

## Your Story Is Your Trojan Horse to Impact

You might be on board with the whole idea of giving yourself permission to be imperfect in public and exploring what being authentic and vulnerable means to you. You might even be sold on why storytelling is such a powerful tool to better connect with your audience.

But chances are, you're still scratching your head as to why anyone would care about your story or how sharing your story is relevant to you running and growing a successful, sustainable and impactful business.

This couldn't be further from the truth. **One of the biggest tragedies is that most people think their stories don't matter.**

The moment you start sharing your story publicly is the moment you start standing out and stop being 'just another company', 'just another leader' or 'just another product or service'. Instead, you provide a face for your company and humanise the experience of doing business with you. Why? Because you become a human being with whom people can relate and connect in a very real way. This enables you to play on a completely different level.

Take Miki Agrawal for example. Miki started three different movements in three different industries in the United States. She built her acclaimed social enterprises, TUSHY, THINX and WILD, to nine-figure companies, wrote two bestselling books – *Do Cool Sh\*t* and *Disrupt-Her* – made the cover of *Entrepreneur* magazine and was named one of their 'most impressive women entrepreneurs' by INC, all while being laughed at by investors, challenged by countless naysayers, and told to be quiet by society.

*Fast Company* said it best: 'Miki Agrawal brings the wit and provocation of a performance artist to marketing products that have been historically associated with shame – and she's catalyzed a movement along the way.'

If you ever get to hear Miki talk then you'll be lucky enough to experience what it's like to be on the receiving end of her raw, honest and powerful back stories of why she started her companies. In short, you simply can't help but be glued to every word she says and feel heavily invested in the positive outcome of her mission.

In public, she isn't scared to talk about having a butt irritation due to a health condition (which led her to launch TUSHY, a take on the modern bidet) or to talk about period-stained underwear (which led her to launch THINX, an undergarment that absorbs your period, a complete replacement for pads and tampons).

She gives us the permission to be unashamed and, thanks to her unique stories, she stands out from the crowd in a big way.

In fact, the most valuable thing you have as a founder, entrepreneur or business leader is your story. And how you tell that story matters. A lot.

And it just so happens that connecting to a story, as you now know, is how people learn, retain information, change the way they feel, and make decisions.

# The Struggle of the Dichotomy

While working with Ali, a very capable, caring and intuitive founder of a fast-growth ed-tech business with big goals to disrupt his company's industry, I realised something strange. The person I was speaking with on a regular basis was very different from the person I was seeing online, especially on social media. Ali's way with words and his energy were powerful, when he gave himself the permission to be real, to share what he believed in and stood for.

But online, the images he shared, the text he wrote, were extremely curated, borderline boring, and just not a representation of what he had to offer.

Naturally, I asked him what was going on. 'I've noticed that in our sessions you're able to open up, share your story and express some really powerful truths, and I really feel as if I get to experience the real you. And I love what I'm hearing not because of the words you're saying but because of how you're showing up. But when I see you pop up on

Instagram or LinkedIn it's as if you're an entirely different person, a cookie cutter version of you. It feels as though it's not you, that you're trying to be someone else. Is it just me or is there something here for us to unpack and explore further?'

Ali breathed a sigh of relief and explained that he sees that, and that he despises social media and has outsourced all of his online content because he feels drained when he thinks about having to do social media.

Because Ali was telling himself a story about what social media was and wasn't, and who he thought he needed to be and couldn't be, he had developed a distaste for all things social media. Ali had decided that in order to stand out on social media you had to have a certain personality. You had to change who you were and needed to love the attention and make it all about how great you were. Which clearly didn't sit well with his values of integrity and his penchant for stoicism. That's why he just wanted to offload the responsibility and delegate his online presence to someone else.

The problem is that in doing that he forgot a crucial part: if you want someone to be your voice then they must first understand who you are, where you come from and what you stand for (or against). He had failed to brief his team on this. They didn't know who he really was, what he stood for, what he stood against, what his true voice sounded like, and what guidelines they should follow. They didn't know what pictures to post or what topics to cover. They needed guidance so that it could feel as if Ali and his team were one and the same voice.

The moment I pointed out the dichotomy between who he really was and who he seemed to be online was the moment he switched things up and started showing up more authentically online. He started to talk about the things that were important to him, the things he was noticing in his industry that he wished were different. He started sharing his personal story, some of his struggles, wins and breakthroughs, and the tools that have helped him run a successful business. He shared why he fell in love with entrepreneurship and making a difference. He started sharing stories of his clients and their success. What shifted wasn't so much the number of likes or shares but rather the quality of engagement he got from people. And, more importantly, how Ali felt when he showed up online: he felt excited.

And, before he knew it, it changed everything.

He started feeling lighter on sales calls with prospective clients or when he delivered work; he felt as though he could show up more at home and be less afraid of appearing weak or vulnerable to others. He started writing more regularly and posting articles he found interesting. And he went back to one of his earlier passions, blogging. He revived his podcast with a new sense of purpose that translated into more powerful connections with his audience and warmer leads for his business.

His team and his clients noticed the difference too. It was as if they suddenly could see the real Ali, not just the mask Ali thought he had to wear to be relevant.

The two versions of Ali became one.

What's crazy is that I think Ali just needed to hear that it was okay to be himself, that he didn't have to be like everyone else he followed online, or that he had to act and pretend to be someone he wasn't.

All he needed to hear was that we wanted the real Ali. The real Ali was enough.

Sometimes that's all it takes, for someone else to be a mirror for us, to reflect back what we deep down so desperately want for ourselves. So in case you needed to hear it today, here it is:

**You have the permission to be yourself in public and to fail in a very public way.**

You have the permission to not get it 100 per cent right, be it the words you say, the way you say your words or the sequence in which you say them. Whatever image you have in your head as to what perfection looks like no longer serves you, it holds you back. I'm here to tell you that embracing the idea of it being okay to fail in public is the answer you've been waiting for to many of your fears.

It's time you show up as your effortless self at work.


# 'I Want to Be Myself in Any Context'

Before they attend my talks, workshops or programmes, most people seem to know what it feels like to be on the receiving end of someone who is inspiring, honest and open in a professional or business context. Whether they've seen it on stage, online, in a magazine, on a podcast, on a virtual panel or in a business meeting, they know that when someone owns who they are and shows up unapologetically as themselves (while still being respectful and mindful of others) and talks about their shortcomings, failures and successes, warts and all, then something magic happens. It's refreshing. It's liberating.

And yet, despite knowing how powerful and engaging it is to do that with an audience, the vast majority of people I meet simply struggle to give themselves the permission to do the same.

As I've mentioned before, it takes a lot more energy and effort to hide than it does to be yourself. Think about it. The time you spend trying to curate the perfect version of yourself for the world to see, the energy you spend trying to control every element of the narrative of what the world gets to know or hear about you and the resources you spend on trying to cover up the real you, is energy, time and resources you could be spending more effectively on connecting and engaging with your ideal audience instead.

I get why busy entrepreneurs and business leaders want help with generating content and managing their online presence, even to the extent of hiring someone to write their posts for them, but a word of caution: short-term tactics and convenience can come at the expense of authenticity, connection and growth, which, in the end, costs way more money, time and energy than you think.

Starting and growing a business isn't easy, no matter how effortlessly people online try to make it sound before selling you a quick-fix scheme to hack your marketing funnels or generate millions in revenue in a few days.

But if building a business is hard work, then building a team is a whole other level of work because it requires a skill that goes beyond just being good at what you do. You must learn how to be good at leading people, with your vision, your mission, your purpose, your values and, you guessed it, your origin story.

## Vulnerability Is Visibility

Adam knows all too well the challenges of building a business from the ground up and scaling a team. Adam, a CEO and founder, came to me because he knew he was operationally sound (he had built a multiple-eight-figure business in a few years), was experiencing fast growth and was now expanding his team. Yet he was aware that he needed to learn how to better inspire and engage his team to help fulfil the vision of the company to change the way people do business in his industry.

What was fascinating was that once I started helping Adam unpack his story, it became clear just how much everything he did and said made sense. He went from experiencing financial stress as a child as his parents struggled to pay bills, to building a booming eight-figure business from scratch.

But that's not what his story is about. It's not about the rags-to-riches narrative that we often get caught up in. No, his story is about an entrepreneur and a business leader who had to learn to be vulnerable and open in front of his team, his clients and his contacts. It's a story about someone who had spent his entire adult life hiding parts of himself because of shame and fear about his past and the impact it might have on his clients, his business and his team. It's a story about someone who feared people would lose trust in him and his ability to do a good and sound job.

And once he started owning his story and sharing it with others, his life and business radically transformed.

When I asked Adam what was different about his experience now, this is what he told me:

'Well, I'm not hiding anything! As in, I'm not trying to hide anything. There were things that were part of my story which I wasn't very proud about, such as losing all my money when I was sixteen or becoming a professional poker player, which I've now told pretty much everyone I've seen since we worked together.

'People have various reactions but it's out there now, it's in the open. It makes me be able to be more authentic. Because it's not something I'm hiding any more, it's not something I'm afraid of any more, it's part of who I am. I'm now sharing things I never really shared with people before. This is who I am, sharing a piece of me. I'm no longer just focusing on what I think people want to hear, I'm now talking about things that I also want to share and talk about. This process has been amazing.'

One of the stories he also shared with me was when he took a new employee out for lunch to welcome them to the team, and during their conversation he shared the back story of how he came to start his company, warts and all. At the next table was an elderly couple who couldn't help but jump in and say how fascinating his story was and how exciting the vision for his business sounded.

He smiled wide when he told me this. In fact, he couldn't stop laughing because he was someone who'd spent his entire life running away from sharing his story and suddenly, in his late thirties, he was seeing the impact and benefit it had on his business, his clients, his team, even strangers. But more importantly, it had an impact on him. It was a sense of relief, a sense of freedom that enabled him to focus on the important work at hand: fulfilling his leadership potential and finally connecting with people.

The added benefit of this process was that Adam was no longer doubting his ability to connect and engage with his team, his business partners or his customers. The energy he once spent on being guarded and protecting his story was now spent on more important matters, like setting the direction of the business and communicating his vision in a clearer and more powerful way which, in turn, eased the onboarding of new employees and helped drive record revenue.

# Courage Is Contagious

*Be as kind and forgiving to yourself as you are to the people you love.*

Dax Shepard, host of 'Armchair Expert',
a top Spotify podcast

Something shifts inside of us when we are in the presence of courage, when we witness someone who, for the first time, dares to open up and be vulnerable. And what I've found is that what you find on the other side of fear isn't judgement, disconnection or certain death, but rather connection, love and acceptance.

Dax Shepard is an American actor, writer, director and host of one of my favourite podcasts, 'Armchair Expert'. When Dax was interviewed on Tim Ferriss's podcast, 'The Tim Ferriss Show', he shared something which I think addresses the fear of what others may think or say when we share parts of our story that we aren't proud of. He explains that having watched for years other people owning up to faults and mistakes, he sees how often their admissions prompt a feeling of empathy and understanding. Being in a 12-step recovery programme himself, he recognises all too well that 'wrestling with shittiness' is something everyone has to deal with.[16]

He then goes on to explain that what he's learned over and over again hosting his show, interviewing some of the world's most famous people (from Barack Obama to Gwyneth Paltrow, Awkwafina to Ed Sheeran and even his own wife, Kristen Bell), is that 'every time you think it's going to be embarrassing and there's going to be backlash, it's almost assuredly going to mean something real and vulnerable comes out, and I have yet to see vulnerability be met with shittiness. Thus far. In general, I have been so encouraged'.

I want to take a moment here to acknowledge that it's very likely most of us have seen vulnerability be met with shittiness at some point in our lives. Whether it was bullying in school, being shot down by a boss, or having a partner twist an intimate confession in the heat of an argument. But what resonates with me about Dax's experience is the overall outcome that has come out of people being brave enough to share something real.

What's interesting is that both Tim Ferriss and Dax Shepard, who each host some of the world's biggest podcasts, give their guests full editorial approval, meaning that before the start of the show, they explain that they will send them a recording of the episode so they can cut out anything they're not comfortable with. This allows guests who may have been burned from previous media interviews to feel completely at ease and comfortable to open up and be real, maybe even for the very first time. This makes for such a rich experience for the listener and gives us a whole new sense of appreciation for and connection with the guests. Because we see them as more human.

And what happens, more often than not, is that the guests realise it's not as scary as they thought it would be, or that the bits they had been holding back are actually the juiciest and most emotionally charged parts of the entire episode.

If you go back to episode 38 of 'Armchair Expert', where Dax sits down with his actor, producer and director friend Jason Bateman (*Ozark, Arrested Development, Juno, Little House on the Prairie*, etc.), you will hear one of the best, rawest and most real moments in all of podcasting.[17] All

I will say is that, for the best part of twenty minutes, Dax and Jason talk at length about a daily ritual we all do in the comfort of our own private spaces but very rarely hear debated in public. At first you'll wonder how on earth anyone could be comfortable talking in public about how they clean their backsides after going to the loo (who knew there were two different and divisive ways to go about your business?), but the truth is, it gives one of the funniest moments in podcasting and also creates an emotional bond between host, guest and listener. It's these rare moments of honesty, of unfiltered truths, that your audience and customers crave. They're what lets them connect with you, to feel less alone and more emotionally involved with you and your business.

## An Open Culture

I've come across an interesting phenomenon in my work: The most highly engaged employees operate in high-performing environments with cultures that allow them to show up as themselves.

I remember spending time with the folks at People Against Dirty, the company behind the Ecover and Method products, sitting across from different teams and asking the same questions about what they enjoyed most about working there and what they found most challenging.

What I was amazed to see was how much they appreciated that they didn't have to check themselves at the door before walking into the office. They were encouraged to keep things weird and be themselves, unlike most of their previous careers where it was an unspoken agreement that once you were at work you switched on your professional self and left your personal self at the door. Which is nuts, when you think about it. How can we possibly expect people to magically switch off all their concerns, worries, thoughts and quirks the moment they walk through the door? People aren't robots. Simply acknowledging the complexity of the human experience can be a huge gift for employees and leaders alike. The good news is that people over-deliver when they feel over-appreciated, and being encouraged to bring their full selves to work is part of that process.

My experience working with leaders and organisations has taught me that *everything* is about story. The stories we tell ourselves about who we are, how we work around here, the spoken and unspoken agreements, the stories we tell about the environment in which we operate, the stories we tell about our customers, our vision, our values, all can be wrapped up in a powerful story.

# Why You Need to Do This (Selfish Reasons)

*I certainly had no idea that being your authentic self could get you as rich as I have become. If I'd known that, I'd have tried it a lot earlier.*[18]

Oprah Winfrey

As Oprah has discovered, sharing your story and using your story can become a way to change the trajectory of someone else's life. And as you can probably imagine by now, be it from a personal or professional point of view, there are many benefits to sharing *your* story, but it can be easy to lose track of how sharing your story not only helps others but helps you too.

That's why I break down the benefits into a few different categories to make it easier to wrap our brains around why sharing your story makes a lot of sense.

## 1. THE BENEFITS TO YOUR BUSINESS

As I said before, when it comes to running a business, invisibility is not a superpower, it's kryptonite. Hiding behind your business is no longer an option if you want to still be relevant in five or ten years.

Indeed, in today's noisy digital world, people are much more likely to buy from people than they are to buy from faceless companies. If you want traction, your *personal* brand will beat your company's every time. As my friend Daniel Priestley, bestselling author and co-founder of Dent Global, says, 'that's because as people we respond better to people than we do to logos, slogans or brands. Humans are wired to trust and connect with a human face over an impersonal brand'.

Many of the people I come across who have achieved traction or a certain level of success in their business have mastered the ability to deliver results for their clients or customers. But what they struggle with is putting themselves forward, i.e. putting themselves out there, especially when it comes to talking about themselves and why they do what they do.

They would happily put all the attention and focus on their team, products or services and clients rather than on themselves. And I get it. If you built a business where you spent the majority of your time talking about yourself and how great you are, you might feel like you come across as a bit of a dick, or at the very least a little narcissistic.

That's not what I'm talking about here.

I'm talking about people who are really good at what they do, who know they can solve meaningful problems for their clients, who have achieved amazing results for their customers and who know they should be putting themselves out there more to reach more people, but who don't.

For whatever reason (and there are many), they despise the idea of having to be in the spotlight, or they don't see themselves as a person who naturally seeks the limelight. They prefer not being the centre of attention. Additionally, they don't believe they have the chops to be as inspiring and as engaging as those they see on stage, in the media or online. And although some may know deep down they have a valuable story worth sharing, most people I come across haven't yet been able to grab the immense value they're standing on, which is, of course, their story.

### Hiding Behind Your Business Is Bad for Business

If we know about you, we are happier to do business with you.

I know many of you wish you didn't have to figure out a way to put yourself out there, that you never had to try to win business and could just focus on actually *doing* the business (while hiding behind your business forever) – you would totally love that.

I also know if you're reading this it means that you have a product, service or message you truly believe in. But I also know you're struggling with the idea of being or feeling 'exposed', that there is a part of you that wishes you could just focus on doing the work as opposed to having to talk about yourself or your business.

If only people would flock to your business without you having to do all the other stuff. Everything would be wonderful, wouldn't it?

But the issue with that is that you're missing the point.

The reason why you feel such a sense of dread isn't the act of having to raise your profile or talk about your personal story. Rather, it's the story you've told yourself about who you need to be or become.

The internal challenges you experience around having to put yourself out there for the world to potentially see, judge or criticise, and be put in the same conversation as others with whom you wish never to be associated, makes it all that much harder for you to believe in the transformational power and healing benefits of connecting with your ideal audience in a public way.

You may also be questioning the real return on investment, and think that your time could be better spent elsewhere.

But if you let me, I'll explain why raising your profile makes absolutely good business sense, how it can be done in a way that feels aligned with who you are, and show you that you get to be yourself in the process.

I'm not in the business of turning you into a performing monkey. Quite the opposite. Finding your voice and finding the courage to be yourself, *your effortless self*, in public is what will make everything fall into place for you.

## Your Story Is the Emotional Glue That Connects You to Your Ideal Customers

Having the courage to share your story authentically can transform your business, change your life and heal the world. It helps all your marketing activities have depth and resonate with your ideal audience, it enables you to gain more PR coverage and media attention, it drives traffic to your business and helps you stand out in a sea of noise, because people are always looking for good stories to share with their audience.

From a business perspective, the benefits of sharing your story are endless as they enable you to attract your ideal clients and push away those who simply aren't a good fit.

### 'My Story Was My Biggest Shame'

Petra Velzeboer, CEO and founder of PVL, grew up in the notorious Children of God cult. 'We were raised from birth to hide in a way because our mission was very much group-think and a group mission of saving the world,' she told me on a video call, 'which meant that any individual story, ambition, flaws were often squashed for the sake of the collective. And so, I would observe that people who had a bit of personality or showed a bit of who they were often disappeared, got kicked out or got punished.' In short, if you dared to speak out, you got kicked out.

She also didn't go to school as a child as the community wanted her generation protected from what they deemed to be negative outside influences. Over time the rules relaxed and she learned voraciously by visiting the local library, hiding books that wouldn't be deemed appropriate. After living a double life, of pretending to be one person within her community and acting out in another way outside of it in order to numb her pain, Petra managed to escape, but not without scars.

By then she had a history of substance abuse, drugs and alcohol, and was pregnant at twenty-two. She had several rock-bottom moments including putting herself and her two young children in danger. Her story of how those low moments led her to start her company to tackle mental health issues is an inspiring story she freely shares today.

But that wasn't always the case. 'My story was my biggest shame,' she admitted. 'I was not always comfortable telling my story by any stretch of the imagination. If anything, I hid it and led a double life. My story was filled with shame and secrets, don't tell anyone, and as long as you wear the mask and pretend that you've got it covered, then everyone will think you've got it covered. Which led to my own mental health crisis, that kind of splitting of identities in a way.'

But joining Alcoholics Anonymous, quitting drinking and practising being honest for the first time while recording her thoughts and feelings was a huge step towards her recovery.

She went on to train as a psychotherapist and gained a masters degree in Psychodynamics of Human Development, none of which would have been possible had she not started to open up and get well.

When I asked Petra if sharing her story has had a positive impact on her business and her team, she was adamant:

*'One hundred per cent good as far as for the business. What's clear as the CEO, and the feedback I consistently receive, is that it informs a very clear north star and vision for the company. No matter the challenges we face, our north star is still focused on improving mental*

*health at work and bringing a positive approach to this space and that mission is very much born of my story, what's worked for me and what I've then seen as a ripple effect work for others.*

*'My team keeps saying that they know exactly where we're headed even in times of uncertainty and I have no doubt that's informed in part by the power of my story which gives permission to the team to be open with their stories.*

*'People every day on LinkedIn are messaging us asking, can we join your team, and it's because of the story they've heard me and my team share. They don't even know exactly what we do at that stage, it's the story that influences the team's story and our values and the overall kind of message that people get.'*

The business impact of Petra owning and sharing her story is huge. She told me that what generates the most business is when she or her team speak with a company's HR person and simply ask how their mental health is, how are they doing? It allows them to normalise the experience of sharing the state of their mental health, the same way Petra normalises hers.

**Dare to Connect with Your Team**

Leila's business was growing rapidly. She was expanding her team and generating more revenue than ever. In the space of a year she went from being a one-woman band to managing over ten employees. But she had a problem. She felt as though she wasn't fulfilling her potential as a leader to inspire and engage her fast-growing team towards a clear and compelling vision. This showed up in different ways for her, mostly frustration at not being able to get her message across clearly when communicating to her team, who seemed to be confused and struggled to connect with her on a human level. She knew she was good at what she did, but she also knew she needed to work around her ability to communicate, relate and inspire others.

More importantly, she wanted to find a way to give her team a reason to trust and follow her into this new, fast-paced lane, to disrupt and challenge their industry. She often found herself having to justify her decisions or spending a disproportionate amount of time trying to rally people around what she was trying to convey, but failing to do so effectively. As a result, she felt as though her team didn't trust her. She knew she needed to change that.

Up until then, Leila was not only unaware that her story was relevant to what she desired deep down, but she had always thought there were parts of her story she should keep close to her chest, that some things are best left unsaid, especially in business. Yet she also knew that something needed to change if she was to switch from being purely operationally sound to being an inspiring and authentic thought leader.

Leila told me that before working with me, peers told her it was hard to trust her, as they simply never really felt as though they knew her. It wasn't that Leila wasn't a good person. On the contrary, she cared deeply about her people, her family, her clients and about reaching her business goals and leadership potential.

The problem was that she had never given herself permission to be vulnerable in public, and she felt that this policy had served her well up until now.

But this left her feeling unfulfilled and frustrated. She knew the impact she and her business could have if only she could find a way to switch things around.

And switch things around she did.

We spent weeks unpacking her story and getting to the root of how she got where she was. This journey down memory lane took us to her childhood, where she and her siblings would hunt for car parts in the woods nearby to sell at a scrap yard. 'My sister started branching out and was our competitor, so naturally my brother and I would go and spy on what she was doing. I guess you could say that at the ripe old age of ten we were guilty of corporate espionage!'

But her story also involved difficult moments, such as having to face public humiliation when her parents' financial mismanagement resulted in them not being able to pay for their meal at a restaurant, leaving the owner shouting at them in front of the staff and patrons.

What's more, we went over the chapters of her life that she had kept in the dark. The parts that she was ashamed of. The part about how, as an adolescent, she lost all her savings, having put it in stocks only to realise it was her fault for being too risky with her investments. Or how she decided to turn a gambling addiction into a profession that enabled her to get paid to travel the world.

Little by little, Leila started sharing her story with the people around her. She was no longer focused on just trying to figure out how best to navigate a conversation by controlling the narrative; rather, she was excited to share stories that she was remembering and, for the first time, owning. In doing so she started to light up, to be more engaging, and people wanted to hear more. Furthermore, at a dinner party, she shared with one of her table-mates a story about how she went from working in casinos on cruise ships, and, to her surprise, instead of people judging her and wanting to run away from her, they got more interested in what she did and shared their own passion for poker, even inviting her to play with big connections in her industry.

She felt a certain lightness, relief almost, as she had spent her entire life trying to calculate what she should or shouldn't say. Suddenly she was inviting people on a journey of better understanding about why she'd created her business and why its core values drove everything she believed in.

Everything changed for Leila the moment she stopped running away from her most valuable asset: her origin story.

## Owning Your Struggles Gives You Freedom and Power

Dave Hollis spent seventeen years at Walt Disney Studios breaking multibillion-dollar industry records at the global box office. Then he quit his corporate job to become CEO of the Hollis Group. He went on to host the number one health podcast 'Rise Together' and write a *New York Times* bestseller, *Get Out of Your Own Way*. In his 'Born to Impact' interview with Joel Marion, Dave said it best:

> *'Nobody wants to have to talk openly about the stuff that we do that we're not proud of. When I started talking honestly about what I've struggled with, the first thing I found was connection. Connection to other people who struggled in the same way ... As long as you're willing to be authentic, transparent and real, owning your struggle gives you freedom and power and connection to others.'*[19]

What Dave's story reminds us is that one of the most powerful effects of this process isn't just sharing your story but *owning* what happened in your life. That's the loophole that turns vulnerability into connection instead of disconnection.

- Vulnerability without ownership = increased risk of the vulnerable details being used against you

- Vulnerability with ownership = power in your story

No one can make you feel embarrassment or shame about your past if you don't first feel those emotions, and part of owning your story is letting go of your own shame.

## 2. THE BENEFITS TO YOU AS A LEADER/ENTREPRENEUR

One of the biggest gifts people discover after finding the courage to tell their story authentically is that people feel they know them without ever having met them. People feel emotionally connected to them and seem to 'get' what they're about and what they're up to. It's as if, without even being in the room, people get to experience them and know what they stand for and what they stand against.

I experienced this bizarre feeling when I was sitting in the reserved row with all the other TEDx speakers at TEDxCardiff waiting for the event to start. As the organisers announced the doors were about to open, I observed the audience rush to find their seats. It was a sell-out event, so it was fun to watch. A woman stopped in front of me and asked, 'Excuse me, are you Mark Leruste?' I awkwardly replied yes, hoping she wasn't going to tell me something like, I'm your daughter. Instead, it was something I never expected.

'I love your podcast and wanted to see you talk live. You're the reason I'm here. I can't wait to see your talk.'

It felt both great and totally surreal. In that moment I realised that this podcast I was broadcasting from the comfort of my small flat in south London was truly reaching a global audience of real human beings.

## 3. THE BENEFITS TO YOUR PERSONAL BRAND

Remember, people prefer to buy from people they know, like and trust. Therefore, elevating your brand by sharing your authentic story enables you to stand out from the crowd and cut through the noise. It also enables people to make sense of why you do what you do. It gives people a bridge to you, to understand what you're about and believe in your ability to care for them and their needs.

It's no surprise, then, that the moment people start sharing their story, people start paying attention and caring about what they have to say and share. It's why bigger media opportunities, bigger podcast shows and bigger partnership invitations start pouring in once you stop being so beige or vanilla.

**Nobody is interested in a flawless, cold and distant leader any more.** Especially if your job is to help people solve meaningful problems, they need to see why you care and why you're the right person to help lead them or meet their needs.

Building a personal brand isn't about shouting as loud as you can or telling the world how great you are. It's about having the courage and conviction in your ability to make a group of people's lives better by sharing what you're up to, what you believe in and what you can bring to the world.

Playing small serves no one, and neither does shying away from your story. So spending the time to learn how to own, share and leverage your story to attract the right kind of opportunities is no longer an option. It's critical to your business success. And let's face it, it's vital to your mental health, too.

The benefits of sharing your story authentically will surpass your greatest expectations, no doubt about it. But one thing that people don't realise is how much it helps attract the right kind of talent to your company or how it can help turn fans into customers and customers into fans.

Take Scribe Media CEO and President JeVon McCormick for example.

## The Modern Leader Who Defied the Odds

Every now and again you come across a truer-than-life Rocky story that just grabs you by the throat and yanks at your heartstrings.

By all accounts, JeVon McCormick is as successful as they come. Husband to a loving wife, father to four amazing children, a committed member of his community, and leader of a fast-growing award-winning company.

But JeVon should have been a statistic. In fact, saying the odds were stacked against him would be the understatement of the century.

Son of a Black pimp and drug dealer and a white single mother who was an orphan struggling to make ends meet, JeVon grew up poor, on welfare and facing pretty much every adversity you can imagine: sexual abuse, neglect, racism, homelessness, violence, hunger, bullying and discrimination.

His father had twenty-three kids, so as early as age nine JeVon was often left in charge of the children, some as young as six months old, while the mother of his younger siblings, a prostitute, was out looking for clients and heroin. It was tough showing up at school without having eaten, getting made fun of for how he dressed, and forced to eat food out of trash cans to curb his hunger. So naturally it all became a bit too much, he acted out and he found himself in and out of juvenile detention.

Unlike those around him, JeVon found a way to get a job instead of hustling in the streets. 'My first job was cleaning toilets.' What set JeVon apart was that even if he was going to clean toilets to help pay the bills, he would make sure they were the cleanest toilets in the whole state.

In his powerful and moving book, *I Got There: How I Overcame Racism, Poverty, and Abuse to Achieve the American Dream*, JeVon shares his past in intimate detail. Today, he is the CEO of Scribe Media, a multimillion-dollar publishing company that in 2018 was named number one for company culture in the US by *Entrepreneur* magazine, and JeVon was recently named Best CEO in Austin, Texas.

As JeVon's website says, 'He's made millions in the stock market (even though he didn't go to college), he was the president of a software company (even though he can't code) and he's currently the CEO of a publishing company (even though he can't spell).'

But the world didn't always know him as JeVon.

At the age of twenty-one, JeVon T. McCormick decided to change his name from JeVon (a name he was given by his mum who had heard it in a French story) to JT McCormick because he figured out early on that 'people would be quick to judge and dismiss me for having a "Black name" like JeVon', he told me. This was sadly the experience of countless other people who discovered that the sound of their name and the colour of their skin denied them opportunities because the business world wasn't ready for names and faces that didn't sound or look like the rest of corporate America.

In an attempt to prove that his name, not his skills or work ethic, was getting in the way of his success, JeVon changed his name to JT McCormick.

He was proven right.

The crazy thing is that JeVon McCormick couldn't get a call back, he told me, but JT McCormick was able to climb the corporate ladder all the way to the top: CEO.

In 2020, two weeks after his forty-ninth birthday, JeVon decided to reclaim his birth name and stop editing himself to make others comfortable. But more than that, he wanted to inspire others who may look and sound like him, that 'there was another way to success than being an athlete, a rapper or a drug dealer'.[20]

The crazy thing is, it wasn't until he started hearing from young kids and their families about the impact his story was having that he realised that it wasn't just about him, but rather about the millions of other kids around the country and the world who feel as though they are alone in their struggle. The only bad thing? It took JeVon forty-five years to share it.

---

If you'd like to listen or to watch my powerful conversation with JeVon McCormick, go to
www.glowinthedarkbook.com/resources

---

## 4. THE BENEFITS TO YOUR PERSONAL GROWTH

The benefits of owning and sharing your authentic story with others go beyond just the business or personal brand benefits. Yes, the more you stop caring about what other people think and the more you find the courage to connect with others through your story, the more it will help you grow your business and become more liked, known and trusted in your industry.

But what most people fail to tell you is that sharing your personal story authentically is one of the most life-changing experiences you can go through. You simply cannot remain the same person once you start opening up about yourself and look at your life through the lens of how it can heal not just others but yourself too.

I recently read a story to my kids called *The Hugasaurus*, by Rachel Bright and Chris Chatterton. On the back cover it describes itself as 'A joyful celebration of kindness and its potential to change the world' while on the inside cover, in the opening section, there's a line that reminded me of something I hadn't thought about before in terms of the benefits of sharing your story. This is what it says: 'and whatever you're feeling, it really is okay – worried, angry, shy or sad ... don't tuck those things away. Share them with another, who might have felt them, too. Perhaps they'll know a lovely way to guide you gently through.'

By opening up about your story, not only will you shift the way you feel about yourself and see yourself in a completely different light, but you will also find others who have gone through something similar or who are able to relate to what you've experienced and can help you heal on your journey.

The more visible you are, the more you'll realise you're not alone. But as you've heard me tell you, this depends entirely on how honest you are willing to be with yourself.

Donald Miller, CEO and founder of StoryBrand and Business Made Simple, who made a name for himself writing bestselling memoirs, says that 'if we are authentic about our shortcomings it forces us to get strong, and if we are inauthentic about our shortcomings we don't have to get strong. We can just lie about it. Real strength actually follows authenticity'.

What I love about what Donald says is that getting authentic doesn't magically make us stronger, but that we have to get strong, which likely means dealing with discomfort and challenges we haven't experienced before. This process enables us to level up as human beings first and business leaders second, and to acknowledge that the discomfort has to come alongside the lightness that comes from sharing our stories.

That's why you always have a choice to make. Do you spend your time and energy and focus on trying to hide, manipulate and be afraid for the sake of feeling safe and having a false sense of control? Or do you spend that time, energy and attention doing what you were put on this Earth to do, i.e. impacting other people's lives?

You can't do both. You can't be real and fake. You can't be honest and deceptive. You can't show up and hide. Not if your intention is to live a life of meaning and purpose, and want business to feel easier, and customers to line up to do business with you, and top talent to rush to your door.

Look at it this way. The more loaded your secret suitcase is, the heavier the journey will feel. If you find a way to unpack and dig out some of the most difficult, shameful and impactful moments of your life and share those stories in some way, they will no longer take up all the space in your emotional baggage.

At the very least, you'll carry a lighter weight, enabling you to run a little faster or walk a little further.

The true gift of doing what you're about to embark upon is that you will see how far you've come and how much you have to offer. That can't happen until you acknowledge your starting line.

The late Debbie Ford, who wrote the 1998 *New York Times* bestseller *The Dark Side of the Light Chasers*, put it this way:

*'We're only as sick as our secrets. These secrets make it impossible for us to be our authentic selves. But when you make peace with yourself, the world will mirror back that same level of peace. When you're in harmony with yourself, you're in harmony with everyone else.'*

### In Order to Know Where You're Going You Need to Know Where You Came From

Despite an award-winning career in her Fortune 500 company, Elaine Carnegie often struggled with self-doubt and low self-belief. Yet she had this story that she wanted to share with the world so that she could help others who were going through similar circumstances.

Problem was, she lacked the belief to move it forward. Or, in her own words, 'I didn't think I was good enough.'

That's when she came to me for help with two critical questions.

The first was, is my story good enough? Is it powerful enough? Essentially, am I good enough?

The second was, is my story going to help others?

Here's what she said:

*'From the onset, Mark's process of unpacking and shaping my story took me on a journey of transformation and self-discovery and made me believe in my story and in myself. Where I am now extends far past my public-speaking ability or my storytelling. It extends into many different aspects of my life. I'm living my higher purpose and I'm really enjoying it.'*

What never fails to amaze me are the before and after pictures of a leader who has taken the time and found the courage to face their story and share aspects of themselves in the service of others and, as a result, clearly position who they are in the minds and hearts of their potential audience.

Elaine acknowledged that it's a tough process:

*'I always get in my own way; self-sabotage and impostor syndrome have been significant obstacles in my life. Like many of us, I have unhealed wounds. Like many of us, I often feel like I don't deserve to feel good or be a success. Actually, I have yet to meet a human being that doesn't self-sabotage to some degree.'*

She first shared her story of burnout, and suffering what she thought was a stroke, on LinkedIn in 2019.[21] Within a day it attracted over 250,000 views.

*'What was overwhelming wasn't the number of views it was receiving but how many people reached out to me personally, having experienced something similar and were feeling so alone.*

*'It helped me realise that yes, my story is about me ... but it's not for me. By sharing our truth, particularly in organisations, we can help others to feel less alone in the challenges they're facing.'*

Sharing her story has led to Elaine and her workplace wellbeing and mental health consultancy business, Being-works, being featured in *Huffington Post, Marie-Claire, Daily Telegraph* and *Men's Health*.

Interestingly, what Elaine said that stuck with me the most was that she finally understood that our stories, no matter how we may feel at first, are equally important to both us and our listeners.

We all deserve to tell our stories; but not only that – others who will benefit from our stories deserve to hear them.

Imagine what it would be like if you could be free of fear or doubt about the value of your story or your personal self-worth. Owning and sharing your story can give you the gift of healing, if you allow yourself to follow and trust the process.

Besides, let's face it. People love personal stories, but sanitised corporate content will never engage and inspire.

# Why You Need to Do This (Altruistic Reasons)

*If you knew how powerful your story was you wouldn't sit on it.*

Andy Henriquez

In 2014, at the ripe old age of twenty, Steven Bartlett co-founded Social Chain. Within five years he managed to get his company listed on the German stock exchange, valuing his company at over $200 million.

In 2020 Bartlett exited his business and, despite being a millionaire at twenty-five, realised he was spiritually unfulfilled. He wrote about the lessons he'd learned in his bestselling book *Happy Sexy Millionaire: Unexpected Truths about Fulfilment, Love and Success*, a lot of which is echoed in his number one UK business podcast 'The Diary of a CEO', which launched in 2017.

Barely a year after selling his business, in 2021 Steven became the youngest investor ever on the BBC One primetime show, *Dragons' Den*.

In a conversation with one of his friends and guests, Dr Aria Campbell-Danesh (aka Dr Aria), Steven shares why he believes that sharing your story is both selfish and selfless, because revealing and discussing your truth is liberating, and selfless, because your humility and willingness to share your experience will help others struggling with their own issues.[22]

## YOUR STORY IS ABOUT YOU, BUT IT'S NOT FOR YOU

The moment you open up and share these difficult stories, the stories that may seem hard to share, be it for what they say about you or those involved in the story, is the moment you realise you're not alone. Think about a defining moment in your life that shaped you for better or worse. Maybe it's a story you'd rather forget, or maybe it's a story you wished more people knew so they'd feel less alone. Usually those are the difficult stories we hesitate to share. And yet, people are begging for authenticity and dying to hear someone else say what they feel deep down but don't have the courage to say out loud.

You can be that person for them. You can be the person who takes a stand and steps up to share something that they're dying to hear from someone else. **If you truly want to have an impact on the world with your message, then you need to understand that, although your story is *about* you, it's not *for* you.**

Your story is a vehicle to connect to those you're trying to reach, not an opportunity for you to make it all about you.

Here's where most people go wrong. When you focus all your time and attention on trying to be in the spotlight, you spend all your time focusing on yourself.

I don't know about you, but fixing all my attention on myself is never great for my self-worth or self-esteem. It's also incredibly mentally draining and can impact my ability to get on with everything else I know I need to do to grow my business. It can literally grind my day to a halt if I pay too much attention to everything that's wrong about me, whether it's how I look, what I've achieved or what I think.

When you're busy staring at yourself, putting all your attention on you, that's when the *Please love me, please like me, please look at me!* syndrome kicks in and manifests as hateful and nasty comments aimed at yourself. And that's never good news if you're trying to put yourself out there to make a difference to other people and, in turn, live a more meaningful and impactful life.

Nine times out of ten, the fear of being exposed or judged resides in the realm of putting the attention and focus on yourself because your attention, your focus, is all on you when you think about what people will think of you.

Trust me, that's where all the insecurities and fears come out to have a saboteur party. (Side note: That's why I hate those fancy round magnifying mirrors you often find in hotel rooms. I've never felt good leaning into one of those.)

If you go back through the list of words and sentences most people come up with when they think about putting themselves out there, you'll notice most of it's about themselves:

*'What will people think of ME?'*
*'Who AM I to talk about this?'*
*'What if I fail?'*
*'What if people make fun of ME?'*
*'What have I got to offer?'*

You get the point. It's never about the people they're trying to reach, touch or transform.

## YOU ARE THE SPOTLIGHT

The metaphor I use is my office desk lamp (think Luxo Jr, the animated Pixar desk lamp character). When I put the spotlight on me, suddenly I feel all sorts of weird self-conscious thoughts. I notice my hair thinning at the front, my beard getting greyer, the wrinkles on my face and the double chin. Suddenly I'm in my own shit and throwing myself a pity party. I'm focusing on me, myself and I.

Basically, I'm naval-gazing. And that's never a good place to be if what you really want to do is go out there, have an impact and change the world.

That's when I shift the lamp towards my participants and say, 'Now that the lamp is directed towards you, what I see is a group of amazing unconventional leaders who are up to some great work but who need help in getting over themselves to share their story and put themselves and their message out there in the world in a big and authentic way. Suddenly I can see all the things I can help you with, all the blind spots you might have about what it takes to do this in a way that actually feels fun and congruent with who you are at your core.'

My ability to switch in an instant from 'Oh shit, how will I look, come across or sound? What if I'm less than perfect?' to 'Wait a minute, I can help these people, I understand the pain they're going through and know exactly what can serve them best right now' is simply a matter of redirecting my focus and attention from myself to others. I often invite my clients to explore the question, 'What would be available to you if you focused on connection rather than perfection?' Abandoning perfection helps us get over ourselves and get on with things. It says, '*I'm not trying to grab the spotlight and make it all about me; I'm trying to put the spotlight on something I care about.*' And I'm not talking about what I had for lunch or most of the other silly things people share on social media. I'm talking about something I really *believe* in. Something I know I can help you with. In the case of this book, I'm trying to put a spotlight on your ability to inspire and engage others by being yourself in public and sharing your story, because I know the gift that awaits you when you do and I know just how much the world needs to hear your story.

By trying to shine the spotlight on a cause I truly believe in, I in turn *become* the spotlight. That's the way you become more known, liked and trusted in your industry without it feeling as though you have to make it all about yourself. When you become the spotlight you take the attention of others and direct it to what you want them to see. It isn't about ego. It isn't about promoting your products or services. It's about standing for something people care about and that you care about too. I want to shine my spotlight on those I know my story can positively impact. I want to shine my spotlight on positive stories of entrepreneurs and business leaders who solve meaningful problems, who are fuelled by purpose and who are making a positive impact on the world.

What do you want to shine *your* spotlight on? Becoming the spotlight enables you to focus your energy on raising awareness about something that truly matters to you. This could be your business mission, it could be a cause that is truly close to your heart, it could be a story that illustrates an important message or it could be sharing some of your client's success stories, or problems you know you can solve.

This could also be raising awareness around something you had to overcome in your life that you want to help others overcome.

The important distinction is that the moment you share your story and show up for others is the moment everything clicks and feels a lot easier. **Most of us find it a lot more comfortable to stand for something we believe in versus having to be the centre of attention and make it all about us.**

Think about it. If your attention is all on you, chances are, you'll resist sharing your story, especially if you're not sure what parts of your story are relevant or interesting to others. But if your attention is on your audience and who you want to reach through the message of your story, then your story becomes the vehicle of a higher purpose. And in that moment it becomes easier to get out of your own way and see your story as a vehicle to serve and connect with others.

This doesn't give you a free 'get out of jail' card to not talk about yourself, by the way. On the contrary, we can use our personal stories to express what we care about. We may feel vulnerable sharing a story of utter failure, and may feel like the spotlight is on our flaws – our naivete, our misunderstanding, our lack of consideration. But we can use the same story to express what's important in that experience – how we found compassion for ourselves, how we became resourceful and rebuilt ourselves from scratch, or how we reached out for connection and asked others for help.

I can't tell you how many times a client has told me that this simple mindset shift changed their life, because suddenly they became excited about the idea of being a vehicle for the change they wanted to see in the world, that it felt a lot more natural than having to shout about how great they were, that they didn't realise they could have the permission to do so.

It's what helped my friend Tony Riddle, a natural lifestyle coach, record-breaking barefoot endurance athlete and author of *Be More Human* (2022) unpack his full story for the first time on my podcast in 2016, back when he barely had a few thousand followers.[23]

Tony has since been invited to share his story, journey and message on some of the world's biggest stages, from the Rich Roll podcast to *BBC Breakfast*, and has been featured extensively in the press, from *The Times*, *The Guardian*,

*Daily Telegraph, Telegraph Magazine, The New York Times* and *Men's Health* to the *Evening Standard* and many others.

Today, Tony has grown an audience of over 70,000 (and counting) on social media and I know for a fact that owning his story and sharing his story and being open and transparent about his shortcomings and achievements is what helps him connect with his audience, grow his business and raise thousands of pounds for causes close to his heart.

It's a transformation I'll never get tired of witnessing.

**YOU DON'T HAVE TO BE THE HERO TO BE IMPACTFUL**

Have you ever noticed how something special happens when we hear someone else open up about their shortcomings? When someone else acknowledges their flaws or shares a mistake they've made or a hard lesson they learned? When someone shares a story of overcoming adversity or getting over something tragic? Not only does it give us hope, but it enables us to normalise our own human condition, our emotions and feelings. We feel more connected to them and, as a result, to ourselves.

It allows us to feel that, ultimately, we are not alone in our struggle here on planet Earth. It's one of the most powerful gifts you can give another human being. It really is.

Nancy Duarte's TEDx talk, 'The Secret Structure of Great Talks', breaks down what all great speeches and talks throughout history have in common, from Winston Churchill to Steve Jobs, JFK to Nelson Mandela. What Duarte realised is that each great speech was built around the same principles, the same patterns and frameworks. 'In reality, the presenter isn't the hero. The audience is the hero of your idea. That's the power of story.'[24]

When American civil rights activist and Baptist minister Martin Luther King Jr delivered his famous 'I have a dream' speech on the steps of the Lincoln Memorial in front of 250,000 people, during the March on Washington for Jobs and Freedom on 28 August 1963, he called for civil and economic rights and an end to racism in the United States.[25] He did so by sharing a vision he had, not just for himself but for an entire nation. He shared his dreams of freedom and equality arising from a land of slavery and hatred. Yes, it was *his* dream, but it was a dream he turned into a universal message of hope, justice and unity.

What Nancy Duarte found in her research was that regardless of the speaker's message, anecdote or story, it was never about them or how great they were, or how everyone should follow them, like them, admire them or love them. No. Instead it was about making it all about their audience and finding a way to invite the audience into their story. About making them feel the spotlight was on them.

The key, it seems, is to find a way to unearth the unifying message within our stories that can benefit others. The good news is that every story, no matter how trivial it may seem, has a valuable lesson. We'll go over how to do that in Part Two, but first let's look at how this concept applies to someone you have most likely heard of.

## TAKE A STAND FOR WHAT YOU BELIEVE IN

Greta Thunberg is a Swedish climate activist with Asperger's who took the world by storm when, in August 2018 at age fifteen, she decided to skip school on Fridays to strike against climate change. She sat in front of her parliament building every Friday holding up a sign reading *Skolstrejk för klimatet – School strike for climate.*

She was passionate about climate change and about doing something to prevent what she saw as a certain doom scenario for the planet – so much so that she managed to convince her family to go vegetarian and adopt lifestyle choices that reduced their own carbon footprint.

Her intention wasn't to become world famous but rather to draw attention to something she believed needed to be addressed. Greta didn't set out to become famous. Or to be praised for helping her family go vegetarian. She set out to save the world.

Suddenly, the press heard about this story and started writing about it. Before long she was talking to big broadcast media channels, her social media following exploded, and people became more aware of her cause and her message that 'Our house is burning'.

At the time of writing, Greta has been featured on the cover of *Time* magazine, has been invited to speak to the United Nations, has a book published with Penguin, is collaborating with Leonardo DiCaprio, has a documentary about her story, and millions follow her on social media.

No matter what you think of Greta or climate change, you cannot deny the fact that the reason why Greta became the voice and face of a movement is because she became the spotlight for it.

Had she made it all about her, she wouldn't have had the same impact.

She was unapologetic about what she believed in and dared to stand up for something she felt needed to be said.

By becoming the spotlight she was able to raise awareness and have a much bigger impact on the world with her message. Because of and as a result of this, she raised her own profile too.

I used to call this mindset shift *Make your audience more important than you looking good*, as in, make sure you put your attention on your audience, not on how good or bad you look.

But my friend Daniel Priestley, who I mentioned previously, said it best: 'Raising your profile isn't about being in the spotlight, it's about becoming the spotlight.'

Hopefully this will give you a sense of relief at the idea of not having to blast the world with your face and wave signs that say, 'Look at me, me, me!' or 'Please like me!'.

Hopefully you'll see this as a paradigm shift; as a tool to help you get out of your own way and raise awareness on something that matters.

Because as much as this might hurt to hear, you playing small and hiding in a corner behind your laptop or your team serves no one. In fact, as you've heard me say before, I'd go as far as saying it's selfish.

Stop being selfish and share your story. Become the spotlight and shine it on what the world needs to know and what your clients need to hear.

# CHAPTER SIX

# The Story Blockers (Personas)

## Imagine Your Worst Nightmare

Back in 2008, when I lived and worked in South Africa, I had an opportunity to hang out with a group of South African stand-up comedians, including Trevor Noah, Loyiso Gola and David Kibuuka. Ever since seeing a live performance in a comedy club, I had wanted to give stand-up a go.

But the truth was, I was terrified.

I kept bugging Trevor and my other stand-up friends with questions like, How do you do it? How do you get up on stage and just make people laugh? How do you come up with jokes that actually work?

And they would systematically roll their eyes and tell me the same thing. *Stop talking about it and just get up there and give it a try. Even if you bomb, trust me, it's not the end of the world. In fact, you need to bomb just to prove you'll survive.*

'Sure, Trevor. Easy for you to say. You could bomb and still have a room explode in laughter,' I replied.

The truth is, stand-up comedy is the pinnacle of public speaking. In order to be compelling and engaging you need to be willing to metaphorically strip yourself naked and embrace all of you, flaws and all. Leaders and entrepreneurs can learn a lot from stand-up comedians.

So needless to say that my paralysing fear meant I never set foot on stage at a stand-up comedy club. Until 2018 that is, when my partner Julie surprised me in front of some of my closest friends with a box full of handmade cards, each one of which contained a clue to reveal my birthday surprise. In the end, I cracked the enigma: You are going to perform a stand-up comedy routine at the Backyard Comedy Club for charity in front of a live audience on 17 June 2018.

My heart stopped. I swear the room's background noise turned into one big fuzzy sound and all I could see were my friends laughing, clapping their hands and pointing their fingers at me.

But a few weeks later there I was, stepping in front of a roaring crowd of over a hundred people. The first few seconds were a bit tricky, as I couldn't figure out how to untwist the microphone cable from the stand. But you know what? I had a blast. As soon as my first joke landed and I heard that first laugh in the crowd, I was hooked. I mean, with the adrenaline and the excitement that I was *finally* doing this, it really went by in a hot second.

Sure, I messed up a few lines, not every joke worked, I tried some morally questionable material; but what mattered was I'd pushed through and, thanks to Julie, who helped me by throwing me in at the deep end, my dream had come true. I had faced my biggest fear and did it anyway. I had responded to the call to adventure. Even if it did take me ten years to finally do it.

Now the back story here is that I was terrified. I didn't want to do it, I didn't think I was funny, I was loaded with self-doubt. In fact, it's safe to say that there is nothing more humbling than realising you're actually not as funny as you think you are. It's a bit like thinking you're really good in bed only to realise that your partner is actually having a stroke. It doesn't feel great.

In the lead up to my live performance I dreaded each session of the stand-up comedy course I was doing. It really was like pulling teeth. I would try out a joke and it would bomb. Everyone else seemed to 'get it' while I clearly was not. My worst nightmare was unfolding: 'Everyone is going to see I really am full of shit.' There was no hiding. Going up on that stage was going to make me feel more naked than I'd ever been in my life. That's why I dreaded it.

But I forged ahead anyway. In spite of the voice in my head yelling 'Don't do it, you'll make a fool of yourself!', I took a crash course in stand-up comedy where I found some allies to help me along on my journey, and then I took to the stage, vanquished my self-imposed mental foes and emerged triumphant and ready to share the lessons I'd learned. It was the hero's journey! I answered the call to adventure, but my odyssey was one of jokes and laughs. The tale was drawn from uncomfortable bits of my real life – my story – and the foes I had to vanquish weren't dragons and orcs. My foes were the limiting beliefs of fear, shame and self-doubt, the same foes that stop so many of us from expressing our authentic selves. I call these limiting beliefs *story blockers*.

# Slaying the Ten Story Blockers

## STORY BLOCKER #1: 'MY STORY WON'T HELP ME GROW MY BUSINESS'

By now you probably know the relevance and importance of storytelling, but you still might not understand how sharing your story authentically is relevant to helping you grow your business, attract the right kind of opportunities and become a magnet for ideal clients or top talent.

But it's more than that. *Your story is the only unique thing about you.* It's your *unique selling point,* or USP. I hate to break it to you, but shy of the people who make up your team, everything else about your company can be replicated.

People can copy your product or service, but they can't copy your story.

Take Lewis Howes, former professional football player, two-sport All-American, world record-holding athlete and current US Men's National Handball Team athlete who also happens to host one of the most popular podcasts. His accolades sound impressive, but his story wasn't all smooth sailing. He says: 'Growing up in the small town of Delaware, Ohio, I overcame feeling dumb, feeling lonely, and being bullied for being in special-needs classes by dedicating myself to becoming the best athlete I could be.'

And his dedication paid off. Lewis went on to play arena football for a season, but a career-ending injury shattered his dreams and his identity.

*'I had nowhere to go but my sister's couch. I was broken, broke and deeply depressed. I didn't know who I was without sports. Would anyone still like me? How would*

*I make money? What will I do for the rest of my life? I'd
never been so lost and afraid.*[26]

Lewis remained sleeping on his sister's couch for a year
and a half, but then she needed him to contribute some rent.
'I had no idea what value, if any, I had to offer the world.'
After a few random jobs, Lewis started reaching out to highly
accomplished people via LinkedIn, and asking them to tell
him the story of their success. 'These "interviews" gave me
new direction, new inspiration and new hope.' They also got
Lewis off his sister's couch and made him feel as energised
as sports had. 'I wanted to share the inspiration they gave
me with others.'

That's why, in 2013, at age twenty-nine, Lewis decided to go
all in and launch his own podcast, 'The School of Greatness',
and start his own business, which at the time was a huge
risk. But his gamble paid off tenfold. His show has now
reached over 1,400 episodes, has received over 500 million
downloads and has built a multiple eight-figure media business. What's even more compelling is that Lewis has openly
shared his story of being sexually abused by his babysitter's
son and his journey to accepting that part of his story and
not being ashamed of it.

The reason I'm sharing Lewis's story is that there are many
podcast hosts out there (more than 2 million of them, in
fact) but there's only *one* Lewis Howes with his own unique
perspective, life experiences and beliefs. Indeed, by sharing
his story, Lewis has managed to build trust and form an intimate relationship with his audience and guests, and this, in
turn, has helped grow and explode his business and impact.
He has become the *New York Times*' bestselling author of
*The School of Greatness* and *The Mask of Masculinity*.

If you're still struggling to see the value in your own story or how it may be relatable to your audience, you might suffer from *proximity bias*: you're too close to your own story to understand what's interesting and valuable about it. To you, it's just your life and it may not seem extraordinary. Someone who hasn't had the benefit of your experience may not see it that way. Get a different perspective, an outsider's opinion, from a trusted friend and you'll begin to see what's been right in front of you all along. When you see your story from a different perspective and see it objectively, then you will start owning the transformational power your story can have for you, your business and your customers.

In today's noisy digital world your story is the only thing that allows you to stand out from the competition and be unique. It's the thing people will remember.

Since the first primitive language-like systems emerged over 2 million years ago, storytelling has been a vital part of sharing and retaining information in order to survive and thrive as a species. That's why we're hard-wired for storytelling.

The way you put a human face to your business is by embracing your personal story. People buy from people they know, like and trust. And it just so happens that storytelling is the best way to emotionally connect and engage with your audience to create that sense of trust with *you*. As previously mentioned, according to Rob Walker and Joshua Glenn's Significant Objects Experiment, the more emotionally invested you are, the less critical you become.

But at the same time as you're starting to understand the power and significance of storytelling to grow your business, and how sharing your personal story can raise your profile and help you reach more people, you're probably fall-ing into the biggest trap most entrepreneurs and business leaders fall into.

## STORY BLOCKER #2: 'MY STORY IS BORING. NOBODY CARES'

**The reason you think your story is boring is because you're too close to it and you haven't unpacked it.**

Most of us don't think our story is interesting, which isn't surprising since we are too busy being in our story as opposed to seeing it from the outside.

We also have a misconception that unless we can turn our story into a Hollywood blockbuster then there's no point in mentioning it. But that couldn't be further from the truth. As Yahya Bakkar once told me, 'You don't need a crazy sob story to make a difference.'

Think about one of your favourite films. Chances are, you probably loved it the first time you saw it and probably still loved it when you watched it a second, third or fourth time.

But now imagine if you had to watch the same film not just ten or a hundred times but a thousand times, over and over again!

Would you still find it as interesting?

Probably not.

It's the same thing with your story. Because you've lived it and know it so well, it just isn't as interesting for you as it is to somebody who hears it for the first time.

The same way a film director might be tired of seeing the film she made over and over again during the editing process and the premiere press tours, for everyone else in that audience it's a treat and a genuine pleasure to discover and experience for the first (and second, third or fourth) time.

After years of interviewing people from all walks of life, I have yet to meet a person whose story isn't interesting.

The good news is that when people unpack their story they suddenly realise they're interesting.

That's right. If you unpack your story and take a helicopter view of everything you've been through, all the obstacles you've overcome, the lessons you've learned and the hard experiences you've lived through and overcome, you'll see just how fascinating your life has been.

An added bonus of unpacking your story is that when you realise your story is interesting, you show up differently in the world. As my CEO client Chris told me, 'I've been amazed at what's come back to me from sharing parts of my story that up until now I had been shying away from. Sharing things about myself, opening up to others and allowing myself to be myself in public, has meant that I'm getting some really amazing responses from some really amazing people. Especially those who matter.'

There's a different energy about someone who fully owns their story, and who knows how to share it in a powerful, punchy way. It's magnetic and compelling.

People who have taken the time to unpack their story are people with a purpose. They know how to passionately communicate why they do what they do. They have connected the dots in a clear and compelling way. They no longer waste their time and energy on the wrong things, like chasing every new marketing gimmick, sharing vanilla posts on social media or throwing a ton of cash and time at sales funnels that don't convert. They are able to effortlessly engage people with their story.

But I also get it. It's hard to pick the right story to tell when you feel as if you have a thousand stories you could share and aren't sure which ones are relevant to your audience. We'll cover that in Part Two, so hang tight.

Picking moments of your life and dropping them in a certain order will make you realise your life is interesting, that you've overcome so much more than you thought and that you're further ahead than you used to be. That was the case for my client Mike, who runs a seven-figure service-based business. After unpacking his story, he realised that not only had he come a long way and was proud to acknowledge his transformation, but some of the stories he had kept hidden were super relevant to his clients and why he was in business today.

Now that you can start to see why not only storytelling matters but also how your story is actually more interesting than you thought it was, you'll probably follow that with a genuine, primal fear ...

## STORY BLOCKER #3: 'I'M SCARED OF WHAT PEOPLE WILL THINK'

If we're being honest, the real reason you haven't taken the time to invest in unpacking, owning and sharing your story up until now isn't just because you didn't know the power of storytelling or felt as though your story wasn't interesting.

It's more likely that you're afraid of what the world might think.

The truth is, everyone has an opinion about you, who you should or shouldn't be, what you should or shouldn't do, say or not say, think or not think, regardless of whether you share your story or not.

You have a choice: keep quiet and play small because you're afraid to offend people you don't care about or care to work with; or stand up and share your story to reach and connect to the people you actually, genuinely want to serve and work with.

Sure, people might have something to say about you and your story, but if you want to make waves then you have got to be willing to make a splash.

Or, as we say in France, in order to make an omelette you have to break some eggs.

The good news is that the same story that might repel some people will attract others.

When Georgie, founder of a service-based company, went through this process, she told me: 'I'm no longer fearing what other people might find out about me.' Furthermore,

*'I've been feeling quite amazed about these recent connections I've had with various people. What's changed is that I'm shedding the layers. I'm just showing up as who I am. I'm prepared to lose connection with somebody on the prospect of creating a stronger connection with somebody else. I'm not fearful of that any more!'*

And that's a really important point. What Georgie realised is that she was willing to lose a connection with someone who didn't matter in order to make a connection with someone who did. Of course, it takes a lot of courage to learn to trust that there will be others out there who will connect and resonate with our stories. In short, at first it won't feel like a trapeze act whereby you leave one connection and gracefully leap to another, more genuine one. Before you see results, you'll likely feel more like you're leaping off the cliff of connection. Even if, deep down, you don't want to stay on the cliff, it's hard to imagine what might catch your fall. But the truth is, it starts with you. It starts with you owning your story so that you're the first person to catch you. That's the power of owning your story and being unafraid of what people might think or say.

## STORY BLOCKER #4: 'I DON'T WANT MY PRIVATE LIFE TO BE PUBLIC'/'I'M AFRAID OF BEING EXPOSED'/'I DON'T WANT TO SHOW WEAKNESS'

Fear of vulnerability is a huge driving force behind people sitting on their stories. This is particularly true when your story involves trauma, difficult moments or emotionally charged events that you regret or wished had never happened. It's hard enough to process these events on your own, let alone air them in public for the world to potentially judge and criticise you.

When a founder and CEO client opened up to me about her story of having lived through a traumatic event when she was younger, I asked if she had ever shared her story with anyone else. She said she had and it hadn't gone down well. Her mum had pointed out that she used to be a happy child but then suddenly something changed, and that she somehow grew up to be someone with a complicated relationship with her body, men, her career and mental health.

That's when she told her mum what *really* happened. She told her about the sexual abuse she'd suffered for many years. Except instead of compassion, love and acceptance, she was met with a sharp question that came across as an accusation. It was in that moment that my client felt profoundly misunderstood and judged. 'I remember thinking, Oh my God, she doesn't understand. She doesn't get it. I felt a profound amount of shame. I felt worse afterwards as I felt as though I had to justify myself. I felt really dirty. That really backfired.'

I wish her experience on nobody and I also know that she is not alone. You'd be surprised at the number of people who carry around some story of shame, guilt or trauma. But what I've learned over the years, both from my own journey with therapy and through hearing the stories of clients, podcast guests and people I meet along the way, is that opening up can be really scary.

Here's what my client told after I suggested she may want to find a healthier environment in which to share her story with someone else: 'I don't want people to know how vulnerable I really am. I don't want to give anyone that power.'

She was primarily afraid of two things:

**1.** Of being exposed: 'I don't want to show weakness. I don't want to take off the armour.'

**2.** Of being misunderstood or judged: 'I don't want people to think I enjoyed it, or had a part in it, or provoked it in any way. I was just a child.'

That's why she found it impossible to share what had happened to her.

But as you'll learn in the following chapters, this process is about finding a way for you to feel safe to open up and connect both with whomever you're talking to and with yourself.

Although the temptation to never talk about these difficult moments is very powerful, as Brené Brown, an American research professor, lecturer, author and podcast host who focuses on shame, vulnerability and leadership, rightfully points out in her 2018 book *Dare to Lead: Brave Work. Tough Conversations. Whole Hearts*, a sense of shame will only multiply when shrouded in secrecy, whereas when talked about and treated with empathy, it cannot survive.

One way to release yourself from a sense of shame, guilt, fear, weakness or exposure is to find a way to talk about it. But first you must find a safe space in which to do so, be it with a trained professional or with someone you implicitly trust who can also support you emotionally while you share it.

The other important thing here is that you're always in control of the information you share. Authenticity is relative to all of us. What may feel like a big stretch to you may feel like a small step to someone else. And vice versa. This isn't a vulnerability pissing contest, but rather the ability to see where we can stretch a little and start opening up in a safe way to eventually no longer be prisoners of our own fear.

However, it's also okay to draw the line of privacy wherever you wish to draw it. For example, Julie and I made a conscious decision not to put our kids on social media. I'm happy to talk about anything that involves me, but not what involves my kids. Although I say I'm happy to talk about anything that involves me, that also depends on the context and setting I'm in. For example, I would only share a story involving a man groping me when I was five years old in very specific settings because it's a story that I'm still unpacking myself and trying to understand as an adult.

Of course, once you start opening up and feeling more comfortable with sharing your story, another blocker may come up: the impact your story may have on those around you.

## STORY BLOCKER #5: 'I DON'T WANT TO HURT SOMEONE CLOSE TO ME'

Here's the thing. Although it's normal to fear hurting those close to us, you have every right to tell your story.

Dax Shepard, aka the Armchair Expert, who we met earlier, talks about how he told a story about his mum on a prime-time talk show. Shortly after the show aired his mum called to say she was embarrassed. He felt bad and didn't realise she would take it personally. But about a week and a half later she called him back and said, 'I was wrong to call you, this is your story. You have a full right to tell your story, and it involves me sometimes, and sometimes I can be embarrassed by that. But certainly, you have every right to tell your story.'[27]

Your story will most likely involve two things: moments you'd rather forget, and difficult moments involving other people you wish had never happened. These are the common ingredients of the most powerful stories because they grab our attention and pull us out of our ordinary worlds. They remind us that we are all grappling with some level of shame and guilt.

Now if the reason you hesitate to share these moments is because you don't want to embarrass or upset anyone, remember that the point of sharing your stories is always about the story itself, i.e. the message or lesson that the story carries. It's not about the people who were involved per se.

Feel free to change their names or make changes to the details of the story to further hide their identities, and don't feel guilty about it. Keep in mind that this has been standard practice in publishing, television and film for decades. In this context, the truth isn't in the details; the truth is in the essence of the story.

In case you haven't noticed, everyone is dealing with something, and as a result of having a filtered version of reality on social media, the world is now gagging for truth. We are all seeking and hoping for someone to be honest and authentic so we can stop feeling so alone in our own struggle.

**In short, talking honestly about your struggles is the ultimate connector. And if you're in business your job is to connect and build relationships with others.**

Here's the deal. Someone, somewhere, woke up this morning needing to hear *your* story. And that could be enough to save a life. I know this to be true, not just through the hundreds of messages we received while I was at Movember, from people who had heard the stories of our community and had managed to catch their testicular or prostate cancer early or found the courage to talk to someone when in need. But also from former guests on my podcast, including Jonny Benjamin MBE, an award-winning mental health campaigner, film producer, public speaker, vlogger and author of *The Stranger on the Bridge: My Journey from Suicidal Despair to Hope*, whose story of being saved from jumping off a bridge by a stranger, and his journey to find him to say thank you, was turned into a 2015 Channel 4 documentary,

*Stranger on the Bridge.* Over the years he's received hundreds of messages thanking him for sharing his story, and I have no doubt that doing so, be it on my show or on many other platforms, has saved thousands of people from taking their lives. But there is a cost to pay for being of service, and that cost is courage.

It just so happens that we all get to decide whether we are courageous or not. And sharing your personal story authentically, in public, takes a tremendous amount of courage.

*There's nothing more daring than showing up, putting ourselves out there and letting ourselves be seen.*

Brené Brown

When you unpack your story you get to choose which stories, and which parts of your stories, you want to share, and with whom. And this can be context dependent, meaning that there are stories that are appropriate and relevant depending on who you're with and what's going on around you, be it in a one-to-one private conversation or in a public setting.

Remember, too, that you can give the people involved in your story a heads-up that you're going to mention them for the sake of a bigger lesson, but keep in mind that I make a clear distinction between asking permission and giving the courtesy of a heads-up. Asking permission means that you are giving away the power of sharing your story to someone else. Ultimately, the choice is yours.

A great example of this was when in 2020 Joe Wicks, aka the Body Coach, shared the story of how he grew up on a council estate with an addict father who was in and out of rehab and a mum who did her best to raise her kids in spite of him.[28] This story felt like such a big contrast to the joyful, energetic and motivating Joe Wicks that the nation and the world had fallen in love with during the pandemic lockdown as he provided online PE lessons via YouTube to help families keep fit and sane. His story sharing gave people a sense that he was human; that he, too, had overcome adversity; that his formative experience had shaped why he does what he does. It explained why he wanted to help people feel amazing about themselves. As he shares his story, your attention is on the young Joe Wicks, and how he and his brother would hear their parents scream and argue through the thin walls, not on his dad who was clearly dealing with his own demons.

When I reached out to Joe Wicks to thank him for his courage in opening up, and to tell him how I shared his story with my clients and participants, he simply replied, 'Thank you for listening, mate. I hope it's helping others too.'

Dr Aria Campbell-Danesh, the high-performance psychologist I mentioned previously, opened up on Steven Barlett's podcast, 'The Diary of a CEO', about how his life imploded the day his wife told him that she was having an affair.[29] But that wasn't the worst part. His wife told him in their kitchen that she was also pregnant with this man's baby and was leaving him.

As Dr Aria recounts this story on air, all your attention and focus are on the emotional pain he must have felt in that moment, not on how much you may or may not be judging his then wife. As a man in a relationship, I can put myself in his shoes and, thanks to narrative transportation, can also feel his pain on a visceral level. Which means I don't have the mental bandwidth to spend too much time thinking, analysing or potentially judging the other characters in the story. Because really, they're not the focal point in the grand scheme of things. Especially as he then goes on to share the rest of his story, of how he ended up healing, and how he uses his experiences in his work with those at the top of their game in the creative industries.

His story is a beautiful reminder that no matter how low we fall or how far down we may feel, there is light at the end of the tunnel, as there's always a way to get better. There are people along the way who will help you and that, ultimately – that moment, that story – no matter how difficult it may be, won't define who you are, but will help shape who you become.

And that's why I share this conversation with my clients who are dealing with Story Blocker #5, as it takes an external perspective to see that when you share a story, people's attention and focus eventually come back to you and your story, not to the other people involved.

Plus, what anyone thinks of you is none of your business. At some point you're going to have to come to terms with the fact that you won't win everyone over. Striving to do so is a lost cause and a recipe for feeling inadequate. Some people will always have a problem with what you have to say or share. Go back to why you're sharing your story in the first place and make that your north star.

Another common issue I hear from people who know they have a story to tell is that they don't want people to get the wrong idea about why they're sharing it in the first place.

## STORY BLOCKER #6: 'I DON'T WANT PEOPLE TO THINK I'M USING MY STORY TO BRAG/MAKE MONEY'

One of the biggest concerns people have about sharing their story is that they'll come across as either self-centred or self-righteous, as if people will think the only reason they shared their story was to make money or to get attention.

The way I see it, as long as *you're* clear on what your intentions are, who cares what anybody else thinks? Don't let the fear of offending a few random people get in the way of engaging, inspiring and influencing thousands of others.

You know why you're sharing your story. And if you're coming from a place of service and connection, then to hell with what anyone else will say or believe. Let them be. Again, what other people think of you is none of your business.

**Simply put, a story not shared does not serve.**

Focus on the people you're trying to reach and serve with your story and message and leave the haters be.

When Rich Roll decided to turn his life around on his fortieth birthday, after years of battling drug and alcohol addiction, it wasn't an easy path to redemption. But the father of four and former lawyer committed himself to healing and becoming the best version of himself he could be.

In 2012, after turning his life around and competing in one of the most gruelling ultra-marathons on the planet, Rich became a number one bestselling author with his inspirational memoir, *Finding Ultra: Rejecting Middle Age, Becoming One of the World's Fittest Men, and Discovering Myself.*

With his story, Rich was able to inspire hundreds of thousands of people around the world, and he continues to do so on his podcast, which continuously ranks as a top ten Apple podcast.

Sure, some people took offence at the way he used his story; to them it may have felt as though he was 'using' or 'milking' his story for attention, but so what. Who cares what a minority think who will hate on whatever you do or say no matter what your intention is? That's why Rich focused his energy and attention on inspiring those who cared and those he could reach.

This is no small feat and it takes time, practice and a lot of self-compassion. Trust me. As much as I'd like to say criticism won't come, it most likely will. When my TEDx talk started racking up views on YouTube, I didn't just get flowers and rainbows in the comments section. People started to personally attack me, make fun of me and say pretty nasty things.

Here's a small sample of some of the lovely comments I received:

*'This is one of the most UN-inspiring TED talks I ever heard.'*

*'This guy will never impact anyone, rather he will discourage everyone ... You're the worst.'*

*'Somebody needs to tell that gobblenut, that hipster beards went out of style back in 2013.'*

*'The thing I don't like about TEDx is when non-comedians are trying to be funny on stage ...'*

I'm not going to lie: at first I was upset. I took it personally. Then I remembered that their criticisms and words said more about them than they did about me. The kind of people I aspire to connect with or associate with wouldn't waste a minute trying to bring someone down.

For me, when criticism (or fear of it) feels like it's shifting the ground under my feet, the best way to anchor myself is to remember that, in the end, our stories all end up the same way: we die. The late Steve Jobs said it best: 'Death is very likely the single best invention of Life. It is Life's change agent.' It reminds me that, in the end, I can go to my grave either full of regrets or full of remorse, and I'll pick regrets over remorse any day.

Besides, someone, somewhere, taking offence is a good sign that your story has power. No one cares about stories that lack an edge.

*Do what you feel in your heart to be right, for you'll be criticised anyway.*

Eleanor Roosevelt

## STORY BLOCKER #7: 'HOW CAN I FEEL SAFE WHEN I SHARE MY STORY?'

In order to begin sharing your story there must be an element of safety. A client once asked me, 'How do I do this without being scared?'

Showing up authentically, being yourself in a business context, and opening up about your story can feel scary and daunting. There's no denying it. And therefore, what most of us seek is some assurance of safety.

Now I would love to tell you that transformation feels safe, and it can up to a point, but the truth is, it rarely does. At least, not while you're going through the process of having to step through your fears and stretch yourself out of your comfort zone.

The word 'transform' has roots in the old French word *transformer*, which means 'to change the form of', and also in the Latin roots 'change in shape, metamorphose' from *trans-*, 'beyond'. Meaning, by definition, a transformation requires you to change, which nearly always requires discomfort.

Together, we will create a safe container for you to experiment with and experience growth by sharing your story in different ways and in different contexts, in your own time. But as John A. Shedd once said, 'A ship in harbour is safe, but that is not what ships are built for.'

In the coming chapters we'll learn how to build up your courage. As with any feat, first we're going to start small, we're going to help you build up your confidence, and it's going to feel a little scary, but eventually you'll overcome that fear and embrace the next step on your ladder to impact.

Despite all of the above, you might be asking yourself if you really want the attention.

## STORY BLOCKER #8: 'WHAT IF I'M NERVOUS OR NOT SURE I'M READY TO LEAVE MY COMFORT ZONE?'

This blocker is at the root of many of our fears. Ultimately, becoming successful and being able to serve a larger audience comes at a price.

**That price is courage, growth and owning who we really are.**

If you embrace what I'm sharing in this book then you will change and you will see your business and your personal life change too. And that might mean some people will feel uncomfortable with the new you. Let them be. If they're not interested in genuinely supporting you to become your best self, then they're probably not worth having in your life in the first place.

In fact, my most popular Twitter post reads, 'The fastest way to upgrade your mindset is to upgrade your environment. And I'm not talking about fancy cars or penthouse accommodations. No. I'm talking about the people you surround yourself with. Make sure you surround yourself with people who *want* to see you succeed.'

That's why it's important for you to do your best to find a community, a tribe of like-minded people who will celebrate you and your courage to put yourself out there and push you to stretch beyond your comfort zone.

As a result, more people will want to work with you or for you, more opportunities will come knocking on your door, and you will get an increase in clients. This can be scary, especially if you find comfort in playing small and flying under the radar. Instead of 'What if I can't cope with the attention I get as a result of sharing my story?' ask yourself, 'Who would be missing out if I didn't share my story?'

Stephanie Slack, a friend and former participant on one of my accelerator programmes, originally intended to start her business as a Corporate Social Responsibility (CSR) consultant for legal firms. She wanted to learn how to put herself out there more and have a bigger impact with her work. The problem was, she was afraid of putting herself out there and was nervous about expressing what she was passionate to talk about. In short, she wasn't sure she was ready to step outside of her comfort zone.

I felt that Steph wasn't really that excited about the work she was talking about. That's when I asked her if there was anything else in her life that she felt passionate about or a pain point she felt called to address. (*Fun fact*: *passion* comes from the Latin word *pati* which actually means 'pain', which explains the title of Mel Gibson's 2004 biblical drama *The Passion of Christ*.)

She replied that there was one thing. A few years previously, when she had been told that her uncle had taken his life, the news had devastated her. She wanted to do something about male suicide but felt as if it wasn't her place to do so. She wasn't born a man and didn't identify as a man; she wasn't a health professional or a mental health specialist at the time, and she felt as though she had zero legitimacy to talk about it.

But while she was busy telling us all the reasons why she couldn't talk about this, you could feel the quality of attention in the room shift.

I simply asked, 'Who here felt that shift in Steph when she started talking about her uncle? And more importantly, who noticed themselves paying more attention to her words?'

Everyone nodded.

'Who here thinks that someone, somewhere needs to hear what Steph has to say?'

Again, everyone nodded.

The truth is, it was the first time I felt we experienced Steph fully, that she showed up with something real, raw, and honest. It was personal.

'Look around, Steph. What do you notice?' I asked.

She took a moment to let it sink in.

'Who here thinks Steph should explore more about this particular topic and that she should continue to share her story about how the suicide of her uncle affected her?'

Everyone raised their hands.

What Steph needed to hear was that it wasn't so much about whether she should or shouldn't talk about this thing that was so close to her, or step outside her comfort zone, but rather how she felt and how others felt when she did.

Steph went on to start giving talks about mental health and suicide, launched a podcast, was commissioned to write an article on men's mental health in *Balance*, one of my favourite free magazines, and eventually was invited to give a TEDx talk at TEDxFolkestone.

I was in the audience when Steph took the stage, and let me tell you, there wasn't a dry eye in the room. It touched us, it moved us. I was moved by her courage to connect with us, with someone who needed to hear what she had to say.

And guess what? Steph's TEDx talk 'We Need to Talk about Male Suicide' has reached almost 2 million views to date.

The crazy thing is, when Steph applied to my accelerator, she wrote in her application: 'I'm afraid nobody will care about what I have to say or who the hell am I to even talk about this?'

Since then, Steph has gained a first-class masters in Mental Health, Ethics and Law and subsequently been accepted onto a full-scholarship PhD programme at one of Australia's top universities, to turn her story into her calling.

Marianne Williamson, a number one *New York Times* bestselling author and former US presidential candidate, famously explained in her 1992 bestseller *A Return to Love: Reflections on the Principles of a Course in Miracles*, that our greatest fear is not that we are inadequate but rather that we are 'powerful beyond measure', and perhaps feel, wrongly, that we do not have the right to be.

**STORY BLOCKER #9: 'I DON'T KNOW WHERE TO START'**

If you want to tell your story and inspire others but don't have a clue how to structure it compellingly or need help in putting it all together, then you'll be happy to hear what I'm about to say.

There's a universal framework you can apply, no matter how unique your story.

Because when you have a battle-tested framework, you'll be able to link your story to what you do, package it for any context, and impact your business with it. And that means any time you share your story, you're creating a potential business opportunity. Sound like a plan?

But here's the thing. Your story doesn't have to be dramatic or extreme. It's about discovering and showing your true self. The you people can connect to. It's about having the courage to unpack the uncomfortable parts of your story or, at least, parts that may feel too scary to share. It's about knowing the real story behind you, and why you do what you do. It's about connecting the dots and making a link between your back story and why you're passionate about what you do. And you have in your hands a book that will give you a clear road-map to unpack, source, own, structure and share it.

We'll get to that in Part Two, and when we do, you'll have a clear structure to help you tackle any challenge when it comes to sharing your story.

**STORY BLOCKER #10: 'THIS ALL SOUNDS GREAT, BUT I JUST DON'T HAVE THE TIME'**

The reason you feel as if you don't have time is because you're busy trying to do all the wrong things to stand out.

As a result, you're spending all your time chasing opportunities instead of letting opportunities chase you.

You're spending time, energy and resources on putting out fires, sacrificing the long-term goals for short-term gains. You're probably also trying to see if posting on social media, spending money on the latest marketing gimmick and trying to find shortcuts to grow your audience will work, when what you *should* be doing is spending time focusing on sharing your unique selling point, i.e. your story.

**Until you learn how to tell your story, well, you'll never stand out from the competition.**

The reason why you're busy trying to grab the attention of your audience is because the world doesn't know who you really are and why you really care and why they should pay attention to you.

*People don't care how much you know until they know how much you care.*

Theodore Roosevelt

When it comes down to this particular fear or objection, you might think of the times you stepped up bravely for a hot second but then your commitment and momentum fizzled out. You might think of the times you wrote a blog post that you liked, and told yourself you would blog regularly, only to keep it up for a week and then stop; or the times you posted something on social media and thought it was fun, told yourself you'd do that more, only to completely run out of steam trying to think of how you wanted to present yourself.

So what gives us momentum? Stop waiting until you feel like it. As I shared with you in Chapter 1, feelings are the last thing to change. Commitment is a much better strategy than hoping to feel different.

If you're tired of chasing business and want business chasing you; if you want to be more authentic and engaging with how you show up; if you want business to feel a little more fun, a little lighter and easier; if you want to be more comfortable in your own skin – then it's time to stop hiding behind your business, and unpack, own, love and share your story authentically to finally become the face of your business and the voice of a movement.

It's time you let the world finally know who you are and what you're up to, what you've overcome and why you're doing what you're doing. Your story contextualises your purpose for others.

# Reality Check

Hopefully by now it's clear that if you're in business, sharing your story is the most powerful way to create a sacred sense of connection between you and your customers.

Because your story is more than deeply personal. It's universal. As James Joyce said, 'in the particular is contained the universal'.

There's a scene in the Apple+ TV show *Ted Lasso* where Ted, a forever optimistic and positive American football coach who finds himself coaching a British football team with zero experience and who leads with nothing but enthusiasm, walks in on Rebecca, the club owner (who also happens to be his boss) doing a photo shoot for a magazine. Ted congratulates Rebecca for this media opportunity, but she is quick to brush off his acknowledgement and tells him the glamorous shoot is not a big deal. That's when Ted reassures her the opposite is true, reminding her that somewhere out there there'll be a little girl dreaming of being a sport executive – who'll see the image of Rebecca and her article, and realise her dreams are possible too.

That's who you can be, except maybe your aspirational audience isn't wearing a purple power suit.

Make no mistake about it, your story has the ability to change *one* person's life, and when it's all said and done, having the ability to change one person's life is enough.

But I get it. Although people who struggle with impostor moments or impostor feelings often do get at least one person who confirms their impact, they often don't believe them, or at least they don't let that feedback weigh more heavily than their own doubts and inner criticism. Changing the life of one person can sometimes feel like it's not enough. But the good news is that we tend to begin to believe our impact when we see it again and again, when we get practice and feedback, and when we see our impact build over time. This can only happen if you start the process and begin the journey to share your story.

# So What Story Are You Going to Tell?

It's easy to feel overwhelmed when it comes down to knowing and picking which stories to share. The good news is that we'll soon discuss a simple framework you can learn to help you unpack your story and figure out what's of value and what's interesting for others, as well as learn how to reverse engineer a situation to make sure you use the most impactful and appropriate elements.

And there are principles to effective storytelling that you can learn and apply immediately in your business and marketing strategies.

Ultimately, the choice is yours. You can either chase your tail, stuck in a state of busyness, constantly wishing things were easier and spending bundles of money on marketing campaigns (which, as you know by now, simply do not work on their own); or you can accept and understand that the only thing that will help you stand out from the crowd is having the courage to put yourself out there with a clear, compelling and powerful *origin story* that cuts through the noise, that people will remember and want to share with others to help you have the impact, income and influence you want.

The voices of doubt, concern and fear will most likely never leave you. I know it's not the most uplifting piece of news, but hear me out: you don't have to wait for all these fears or blockers to magically disappear. Instead, acknowledge their existence, and decide whether you will let your story blockers win or if you will conquer your story blockers.

# CHAPTER SEVEN

# Your Origin Story – Your Million-Dollar Asset

Here's a question: what do Batman, Oprah Winfrey and my local independent guitar shop have in common?

They all have an origin story.

You also have an origin story and it is one of the most powerful secret ingredients you possess, one that weaves everything together and helps your audience connect instantly with who you are and what you do.

The concept of an origin story is typically associated with the entertainment industry, especially comic books and the films and television shows based on them. It's the background story that explains how a character got from their point of origin to their destination, explaining who they became along the way and why they behave the way they do. One of the most famous superhero origin stories is that of Peter Parker, a bookworm with a love of science who is teased by his schoolmates. Peter is bitten by a radioactive spider, giving him the proportional strength, reflexes and wall-climbing ability of a human spider, and turns into Spider-Man, but soon afterwards, he ignores the opportunity to apprehend a burglar. When his Uncle Ben is murdered by the very same thief, Peter has a tremendous sense of guilt and feels responsible for his death and for making his Aunt May, now his sole parent figure, a widow. Peter learns a lesson that sets the tone for the character's sixty-year run:

*With great power there must also come – great responsibility!*

That, in a nutshell, is Spider-Man's origin story.

Switching from Marvel to DC, the 2005 film *Batman Begins*, starring Christian Bale and directed by Christopher Nolan, devoted its entire running time to a deep dive into Bruce Wayne's back story: how he witnessed his parents' brutal murder and learned the arts of fighting, eventually to return to Gotham City to fight injustice. It's one of my favourite Batman films because it gives us a different dimension to Batman, a certain edge or a dark side to why he is who he is.

What I love about origin story-based narratives is how those who write and create them attempt to give us a glimpse into the psychological and emotional make-up of a character, be it a hero or a villain, to better connect us with who they are, and to help us become emotionally connected to them.

Politicians understand this very well. Their goal is often to craft and manufacture (at times) a compelling back story explaining why they care and why they're the right candidate to lead.

Origin stories are also important in court when a defence lawyer makes the case that their client, no matter how hideous their crime or how guilty they may appear to be, is sympathetic. They do this by painting a picture of what their life was like growing up, describing in great detail the abuse, neglect or tragedies that shaped their upbringing, all with the hope of triggering an emotional response in the judge or jury.

When we understand the circumstances behind someone's behaviour, we can make more sense of it (although we don't necessarily have to agree with it).

Take the Joker, Batman's arch-enemy. Until recently, the Joker, although played by charismatic actors like Jack Nicholson and Heath Ledger, was a character who came across as simply deranged and evil. This changed in 2019 with the film *Joker*, directed by Todd Phillips, with Joaquin Phoenix in the title role (he subsequently won an Academy Award for his performance). *Joker* shares the intimate, painful and uncomfortable journey of Arthur Fleck, a poor struggling clown suffering from mental health issues who becomes the unwitting leader of a movement to put an end to Gotham City's unequal distribution of wealth. Through a history of abuse, neglect and bullying, Arthur Fleck becomes the Joker.

It's a fascinating film because you can't help but feel sorry for the character (even though you know what he's about to become) and have empathy for someone who clearly has gone off the rails. That's the power of an origin story.

You might not be a superhero or a criminal mastermind, but trust me when I say that an origin story will work just as well for you as it does for them.

## Turn Your Pain into Your Purpose

*All the superheroes we love and worship all got their powers from something bad happening to them.*
Jay Shetty, author of *Think Like a Monk*[30]

One thing most origin stories have in common is that the trigger that caused the protagonist or antagonist to gain their superpowers, more often than not, is a place of pain. Something tragic or something challenging occurred that forced them into a course of action or otherwise motivated them to do something. We're rarely introduced to a character who has a beige or vanilla background story, where everything was perfect, and the only reason why they are who they are is, well, just because.

We just wouldn't buy it, or worse, we wouldn't care. It wouldn't be particularly interesting. We'd switch off and disconnect.

But when we connect a moment of pain, injustice, frustration to a bigger purpose, to why we do what we do, that's where the fireworks of connection go off. Origin stories are made up of the moments that *change* us, they set us on new paths to new destinations, and we're not the same person at the end as we were at the beginning, perhaps changing from a victim's mindset to a hero's mindset. It makes sense. Those moments of pain and injustice, those points of decision and change, become ingrained in the heads of our audience. We're not trying to con them or convince them of something we don't feel particularly connected to; we're not just doing it to make a quick buck. We feel connected to what we're sharing because our origin story made us who we are. It can change your audience, too, as it can help them discover or reconnect to their own origin stories, no matter how scary or daunting that may be.

This origin story concept isn't exclusively for entertainment. It can be applied in business too. In fact, understanding your origin story is key to attracting the right people.

**TAKE OPRAH WINFREY**

Oprah Winfrey was born into poverty to a single teenage mother, was raised by an abusive grandmother, and from the ages of nine to twelve was repeatedly assaulted and raped by a nineteen-year-old cousin. At thirteen, after years of abuse, she ran away from home. At fourteen she was pregnant. Her son was born prematurely and died shortly after.

She eventually went to live in Nashville, Tennessee, and landed a job in radio while still in high school. By nineteen, she was a co-anchor of the local evening news.

You probably know the rest of the story. Oprah's career continued its upward trajectory and *The Oprah Winfrey Show*, the highest-rated television programme of its kind in history, ran for twenty-five years and recorded over 4,561 shows. She is often ranked as one of the most influential women in the world.

Looking back at Oprah Winfrey's life, it's easy to see how her superpower – to relate to and have empathy with others – is deeply rooted in her difficult upbringing and having to overcome so many obstacles and struggles. The depth of her connection with her guests is palpable. She has the courage to share her life with the world; she is able to be fully present with those who feel shame, guilt or pain. And if you ever doubt your gifts, remember that Oprah was removed from her first news anchor position because she became *too emotionally involved* in her stories, the very quality that became the key to her eventual success.

# Connect the Dots

The deeper purpose of sharing your story is so you can stand in your truth, claim it, and live it – and through sharing it, help others develop the tools and courage to do the same.

The other added benefit of sharing your story is that your origin story is a great asset to attracting your ideal customers and it's key to attracting the right opportunities. Just as with superheroes or villains, your audience wants to know why you do what you do. They want to know if what you do means something *real* to you, that you're in it for the right reasons, that you're not just chasing an opportunity. It enables your audience to build trust with you, which is the foundation of any healthy relationship.

Although many successful entrepreneurs and business leaders have been shaped by trauma and difficulty, you don't need to have a dramatic story to make a difference.

**MEET THE GANGSTA GARDENER**

*Growing your own food is like printing your own money.*
Ron Finley

Ron Finley's story is an incredible reminder of what can happen when we fight for what we believe is right and try to bring people together for a greater cause – in his case, to change his community.

Ron Finley goes by the name of the Gangsta Gardener because he believes there's nothing more gangsta than growing your own food. In his 2013 TED talk, 'A Guerrilla Gardener in South Central LA', Ron shares his story of how living in a food desert, where 'the drive-thrus are killing more people than the drive-bys', led him to start planting vegetables and fruit on abandoned plots of land, the central reservations of highways and the curbs and verges of roads in the city where he'd grown up and raised his kids.

He was tired of seeing the alarming statistics showing how obesity and preventable diseases were killing his community, as well as having to drive for around three-quarters of an hour to find an apple that wasn't impregnated with pesticide.

So Ron planted a food forest outside his house. His group of volunteer friends grew this incredible food sanctuary to help feed the community, for free, by repurposing abandoned sidewalks and turning them into fountains of fresh food.

Sadly, he received a citation from the city saying that he had to destroy his garden or face legal action.

But Ron wasn't having any of it. Not this time.

His story ended up being featured in the press, and he and his friends gathered over nine hundred signatures on a petition on Change.org.

He was allowed to keep his project and, today, Ron sees gardening as both art and activism. His soil is his canvas. His garden is a tool for change in the community. It's a way to transform the soil we live on and educate others about the importance of good nutrition.

'You'd be surprised at how kids are affected by this. Gardening is the most therapeutic and defiant act you can do, especially in the inner city. Plus, you get strawberries ...'

Seeing how gardening was changing his entire community, Ron knew he was on to something. That's when his team of volunteers started planting gardens in homeless shelters around his community.

*'If kids grow kale, kids eat kale! If they grow tomatoes, they eat tomatoes. But if they're not shown how food affects the mind and body, they'll eat whatever you put in front of them ... I want to plant a whole block of gardens, I want to take shipping containers and turn them into healthy cafes. Putting people to work and getting kids off the street and teaching them the honour and pride of growing your own food ... If you ain't a gardener, you ain't a gangsta. Be gangsta with your shovel, let that be your weapon of choice.'[31]*

As you hear Ron share his story, be it in his TEDx talk or his masterclass, you can't help but root for his cause and want to support him in whatever way possible, as well as just grab your shovel and start planting. And what I also like about Ron's story is that it's a good example of a story that doesn't involve a deep personal trauma, in the traditional sense, and yet it still works.

Don't get me wrong, the food deserts in the US are a very real problem. There are many parts of America where grocery shopping happens at the gas station because that's the only store available within a community. In inner cities, this disparity can often be traced back to racist urban development policies. Ron's urban gardening is a heroic response to a very tragic condition.

## Make Them Care

Here's what my friend Daniel Priestley, who I've mentioned previously, shared with me about why sharing your story isn't just a nice thing to do but a vital business skill to master:

'The reality is that most people who meet you for the first time have a certain scepticism or assume that if you're talking about something exciting to you and they don't know you, you are just purely and simply chasing an opportunity or trying to ram it down somebody else's throat. What you need to do, especially if you're starting or launching something new, is to establish your credentials as to why you should be talking about this in the first place. You want to tell your origin story quickly and powerfully so that people understand that you are not Johnny-come-lately to the industry, you're not someone who's opportunistically chasing money, you're not just simply after the next big thing purely because you think it's a good way to make a quick buck. It's not some quick opportunity that you've spotted.'

In other words, sharing your story enables your audience to make sense of why you're the perfect person to be doing what you're doing because you've made it clear that you're in it for the right reasons and you have skin in the game. It also enables your audience to understand that you have both empathy and credibility which, in turn, also build trust. That's what a valuable origin story should do for your audience: make them understand why you're doing what you do in a really quick and simple way and make it clear why you're the right person to help them fix their problem.

There are countless opportunities for you to share your origin story. In fact, you'd probably be amazed by how many opportunities you've missed, from introducing yourself on a speaker panel, on a podcast interview, on an interview with the press, addressing new team members, pitching your business to potential investors, delivering a keynote, running a training workshop or speaking on a one-to-one with a potential client, to introducing yourself at a networking event when you're asked what you do. The opportunities are endless.

As you will learn in Part Two, there is a way for you to craft a short, digestible story so that you can make the most of the question, 'What do you do?'

# This Isn't Your Wikipedia Page

The difference between a full-length, two-hour blockbuster movie and you sharing your story in a business setting is that you won't have two hours to develop your back story for your audience to understand what you're up to and why. You need to share your origin story in a clear, punchy and succinct way while having the courage to dig deep and find the theme, the narrative thread, that has shaped you. And finding that narrative thread often begins with pinpointing a formative event in your past.

One of the biggest problems people wrestle with when it comes to pinpointing the moment or event that defined their trajectory towards doing what they do today is the feeling that they don't know where to start or that because their life is so full of twists and turns and many different experiences, they can't possibly come up with a clear origin story narrative.

Nothing could be further from the truth.

Typically, when you go through the process you're about to go through, and map out your entire life and draw out all the different stories that have been significant to you in one way or another, you'll find that, even though it seems you've done lots of different unconnected things, you'll start to see a theme. You'll discover something that most likely took place when you were between the ages of six and twelve that has shaped your destiny, guiding you to your lifelong passion, the passion you still pursue today.

Sometimes this event is as clear as day, and sometimes it takes a little bit of time and work to unpack it, but it's there. It always is. And when you find it, it will give birth to your million-dollar story. The trick is to learn how to pick the bits of your story that support the business or the work you're doing today. We'll dive more deeply into this later in Part Two of this book, so don't worry, but for now, the important thing is to know that the trick is to reverse engineer your story in order to look for the common theme or trend that supports why you do what you do. And zone in on that part of your story.

Before we move to how to do that, I want to share a powerful example of how a life event can not only shape the rest of your life but also help you make sense of yourself.

## Add Your Flavour

On 25 May 2020, George Floyd's murder by a Minneapolis police officer in eight minutes and forty-six seconds was captured on camera, and the world broke out in shock and anger.

What followed was a social media storm that attempted to raise awareness (yet again) about historical and systemic racism not only across the US but around the world. While well-intended individuals and organisations posted black tile images on their social media feeds in protest, and used hashtags to raise awareness, much more was needed to address the bigger issue. Some decided to focus on practical issues by providing support and direction to help others do the right thing and be part of the solution.

One of those individuals is Vanessa Belleau, a French Caribbean woman who has called London her home for the past seventeen years. She is the founder of High Fifteen, delivering future-proofing insights and diverse strategies to businesses along with executive coaching to individuals.

Thanks to an honest and vulnerable approach, a joyful nature and her #TeamTooMuch personality, Vanessa is an in-demand diversity, inclusion and belonging consultant for SMEs and major brands such as Givenchy, Louis Vuitton, Gymshark and Nestlé.

When Vanessa shared her story with me, I was gratefully reminded of the emotional cost that comes with doing something you believe in.

On the outside, Vanessa's branding is all about joy and being colourful. But it's easy to forget that making waves is a double-edged sword, as navigating the discomfort of difficult conversations around race and identity at large can bring out a lot in people, and that means having to carry a lot of baggage that isn't yours.

'I still see myself as the three-year-old Black girl who realised at that age that society wasn't made for her,' she told me. The middle child in her family, Vanessa was born with twelve fingers (as was her father). The extra fingers were removed, but a bit was left behind. 'When I went to nursery, we were playing this game called *La Tomate* where you're meant to hold each other's hands. But other kids didn't want to hold my hand because I was different. Not because I was Black but because I had an extra bit of skin on my hand. In Caribbean culture, having twelve fingers is a sign of good luck. But at that moment it didn't feel that way.'

As Vanessa started to discover she was 'different' at school so she started to notice things about society more broadly. 'As I had more experiences in life, and grew up, as a girl I became conscious that I'm not the same or seen the same as boys,' she continued. 'Then as I grew up I started to get the notion of being Black. When I was at the swimming pool in Germany, white kids were fascinated by my hair and would run up to me and touch my hair, petting me as if I was a monkey, pulling on my braids. I was like, "What is this!?"'

When I asked Vanessa if she remembered her earliest memory of feeling different because of her skin colour she shared a story that captures the very essence of why I wanted to write this book for you.

Here is her story in her own words:

*'Oh, I remember. It was in Germany, Bavaria. I was twelve years old. And it's the most blatant one that comes to mind. My dad was in the police force in France so he had an opportunity to send me to a German holiday summer camp for three weeks. Once all the children arrived in Germany the way the organisers planned out the match-making process between the young students and hosting families was to line up the kids on one end and create some sort of celebration ritual to meet and greet each kid. They would go something like, "Hi, this is Mark! Mark is twelve years old, he's from Paris," and so on, and then say, "So who would like to accept Mark in their house?"*

*'Families would then be like "yes great!" And the children would then join their hosting families.'*

Except, when it was Vanessa's turn to step forward, nobody said anything.

*'I was the last child in line. Nobody said I would like Vanessa. I was the only Black child. My dad always told us, preparing me and my sisters for life, that, "Hey, you're going to be the grain of coffee in a bowl of milk. That's going to be you. But you know what? Add that flavour. Add that strength." That's the type of parents I have.'*

Unfortunately, Vanessa's parents weren't there to remind her of her greatness as she stood there, alone.

*'My parents didn't know they were sending me to a racist experience. I was like, "Oh my God, so that means that nobody really wants me here. What am I going to do? Am I going to live with the teachers?"'*

Thankfully, there was a family who came a bit late to the so-called Celebration of Arrivals, and they picked Vanessa.

*'Thankfully I ended up with them. Turns out my "foster" mum was a mixed-race French lady, lived in Germany and came from Guadeloupe, where my mum is from, and had the same name as my mum. At first she asked me in German what the weather was like, but once she saw the look on my face, she switched to French. That's when I smiled. And what I know today is that in every moment you can find those little lights that give you hope.'*

I wouldn't wish Vanessa's experience on anyone, and yet that experience, coupled with all her other life experiences, including being rejected by her three-year-old peers in the playground at nursery, beautifully positioned and shaped

Vanessa as the perfect person for companies to bring in to talk about diversity, belonging and inclusion.

Because in that moment, as Vanessa shared her experience of being alone, as the only Black child in line and feeling utterly rejected by everyone, my heart sank. I was moved. Vanessa was moved to tears too as she recounted her experience, and in her story I felt her essence, her truth, her *why*. There wasn't a shadow of a doubt that she absolutely would be able to relate to the pain points her clients experience navigating through the tricky waters of diversity, inclusion and belonging.

The more we understand our own pain and develop the skills to work with it, the more available we are for compassion and empathy with others. Chances are, most of us can tell the difference between someone who is sympathetic and someone who is empathetic. A sympathetic person is understanding and kind, but doesn't actually hold the emotional energy of the experience with you. An empathetic person holds that energy, and models how to hold it with compassion.

After hearing Vanessa's story you may think it's obvious why she does what she does, but you'd be wrong.

'People had to convince me to do this work,' she told me.

Indeed, up until then, Vanessa had spent her entire career as a consultant specialising in business strategy. From diving into market research, brand competitiveness, future trends or innovation, she was good at what she did and happy with it.

She worked at a future-trend think-tank agency and travelled the world speaking on the future trends that would impact the design industry, widening the perspectives of a lot of clients. One day Vanessa was invited to join a panel to talk about the future of sustainability. She was the only

Black woman on the panel and she soon found herself talking about sustainability and *diversity*.

Kate, a very senior member from Levi's, was in the audience. It just so happened that Levi's was organising a leadership summit for women and was looking for a keynote speaker to inspire their people by talking about their career, aspirations and more. Would Vanessa be interested?

Vanessa was quick to reply. 'Sorry, I don't do that. If you want me to talk about the future of something, no problem, but I can't talk about my past or future.'

Kate said, 'No, we would like you to come in and talk about yourself, your achievements as well as the barriers you've overcome.'

'Listen, my life is my life,' Vanessa insisted. She told me, 'Not only had I no idea about personal branding but I didn't see how my personal story was relevant to anybody else but maybe my family.'

But Kate was tenacious and convinced Vanessa that her story had value.

'What can I tell them to actually make them care about what I'm going to say?' she wondered.

It was a personal challenge as, despite her appearance and bubbly character, Vanessa was actually dealing with a hefty dose of self-doubt and having a massive impostor moment. She didn't know how sharing her story could inspire 120 women at a conference. Up until then, Vanessa had never used the word *I* in a presentation. She had always used the word *we* since she was representing other agencies. That's why talking about herself felt so alien to her.

But she also knew it was a great opportunity to test the waters of being a freelance consultant. She took the stage and kicked off her presentation with her baby picture on the giant projection screen (which went down a treat). Despite her resistance and fears, she shared her *whole* life story, the good and the bad moments, her unconventional career, and how she ended up doing the work she did. She wanted everyone in that audience to know they didn't have to be pigeonholed into one career, that they could follow their own path, that it's okay to reinvent yourself and chase what brings you joy.

She got a standing ovation.

Afterwards, Vanessa found a line of women waiting to ask her if she'd be willing to coach them.

'The human connection there, that happened after me showing up as the real me on stage, was massive. I was so nervous!' she said.

There's a part of all of us that resonates with people who are brave enough to be who they really are in public, who embrace themselves, flaws and all, and who are brave and generous enough to share their true story with us too. Because deep down we yearn to have the same courage for ourselves, and in seeing someone stand up and step up we feel that calling a little bit more.

Over the two days of the summit, Vanessa was told that her speech had really resonated with the women in the audience, and Levi's asked Vanessa to deliver workshops to help their teams with mindset, resilience and changing their culture. That's when Vanessa started her new direction towards becoming a diversity, inclusion and belonging consultant and an accredited executive coach. It all started with someone convincing her that her message mattered and her story had value. It started with Vanessa having the courage to believe that someone, somewhere could benefit from hearing her story to be either inspired or find hope in their journey too. It started with Vanessa finally having the courage to publicly share her amazing and heart-breaking *origin story*. It continued with her studying and learning new skills and insights to support businesses and people with marginalised experiences, in their efforts to belong more.

And when she did, everything suddenly fell into place, turning her story and perspectives into a six-figure business. Funny how things work out when we stop running away from our history.

# Zoom Out

Hopefully, by now you're excited and ready to dive deeper into unpacking your story and finding the gems that will help you better connect to your ideal audience by sharing your origin story too.

In order to do that, though, we need to zoom out draw all the different important elements of your story so we can spot the theme, and then pick the elements of your story that tell us in a simple way why you started your business in the first place, and why we should care and believe that you care too.

*Let's begin.*

# PART TWO

# How to Unleash Your Story

# CHAPTER EIGHT

# The Process: An Introduction

## From Shame to Service

In the summer of 1991 Shaka Senghor shot and killed a man. He then spent nineteen years in prison, seven of which were in solitary confinement in a room smaller than your bathroom. He was eventually released in 2010 and went on to speak out about the broken US justice system, turning his story into a powerfully compassionate human movement.

Despite being convicted of murder, Shaka Senghor today is the head of diversity, equality and inclusion at TripActions, Director's Fellow alumni of the MIT Media Lab, a college lecturer, TED speaker and a *New York Times* bestselling author. Oprah Winfrey said her interview with Shaka was one of the best conversations she's had.

Do you think Mr Senghor felt a little reluctant to share his story? Wouldn't you?

From shame to service, whoever you are, or whatever you bring to the table, I promise you, this will work.

At the start of this book I made a promise to you, that if you were open and willing to be coached, if you trusted the process and if you showed up and did the work, you would experience a significant shift or go through a meaningful transformation of feeling confident sharing your story authentically in public, with others, no matter the setting or context.

I intend to keep my end of the bargain, and it begins with introducing you to a framework I've developed that has yielded extraordinary results for my clients and for me, and that soon will for you.

In a nutshell, what you're about to learn is a process that will help you go from *I don't see how my story matters* or *There's no way I could ever share my story in a professional setting* or *I can't see how I can make sense of all the different bits of my story* to *I can't freakin' wait to share my story!*

What's interesting is that while I was hearing about all the struggles people have with putting themselves out there, I was also interviewing hundreds of inspiring guests who dared to be different by being vulnerable, honest and authentic in public.

That's when I realised I was in an extremely privileged position. Like the chair umpire at a tennis match (you know the one, she usually sits on top of a freakishly tall chair and is responsible for calling the score and upholding the rules of tennis), perched high up and able to see the whole picture, I could see what truly separated these two groups.

On one side I had a group of people who were stuck in fear but wanted more of what the other group of people who chose to share their story had, but who were stuck in the starting blocks. And on the other side I could see people who had somehow found a way to sprint beyond the same limiting beliefs. I could clearly see what was getting in the way and what was needed to help those who were stalled to finally begin their journey around the track.

So I started testing and trying different tools, exercises, frameworks and methodologies with my private one-on-one clients and group coaching participants, applying what I was learning from speaking to high performers, to see what worked and what didn't.

And it turns out there's a method to the madness.

## Why My Process Works (When Others Fail)

After speaking with hundreds of impact-driven leaders about what was missing on this journey, I discovered that there was a major ingredient that too many people overlook: the fear of being emotionally exposed when opening up about yourself in public.

That was the missing ingredient.

It wasn't so much the 'am I good enough' but rather the 'what will people think or say' that was getting in the way.

I needed to find a way to create an environment for my clients that was conducive to having a sense of emotional safety while also providing a clear road map to reach their desired outcome.

The first step was to establish confidentiality. As an accredited International Coaching Federation (ICF) professional coach, I am required to hold all shared information as confidential (unless clients talk about harming themselves or others, in which case I must notify the appropriate bodies). This helps my clients feel safe to open up to me.

As you unpack your story, remind yourself that you are always in control of who gets to see or hear what you are writing down. You could share it now, you could share it later, or you might never share it at all. At this point, the process is for your eyes only, so let yourself be real, honest and open. Let it rip.

The second step was to design an alliance with each client to make it clear that this is a process, a journey, and that it's okay to feel reluctant to open up about certain aspects of their life. I make it clear that I'm not here to force them to share anything that makes them feel uncomfortable. My mission, rather, is to help them unpack their story first and foremost, for themselves, so they can look at their history from a new perspective that minimises fear, shame, guilt and confusion. My promise is always to approach their story with curiosity, empathy and a lack of judgement. I invite you to do the same with yours. Imagine that one of your best friends is sharing their story, and they are afraid to do so because of how they feel about it. How would you want to make them feel? Make sure to treat yourself with the same compassion and empathy.

The third step was to explain that the process I had developed, the road map I was about to share and the journey I was going to take them on, has helped countless other clients who felt just like they do transform into genuine, authentic leaders. This helps to normalise the process so they don't feel alone in their struggle to be more themselves in public, or to open up more about their true story on a bigger stage. They know they are in good hands. If you find yourself thinking that surely you're the only person in the world to struggle with your history or parts of your story, remember my words: *you are not alone.* The voice you hear is your inner critic holding you in its grasp to keep you safe and comfortable.

Finally, I made sure to open up about *my* shortcomings, share some of the things that I'm not proud of, moments that nonetheless shaped me to become the leader I am today. Leading with vulnerability enabled *them* to follow with authenticity.

## How It Works

*In the beginner's mind there are many possibilities, but in the expert's there are few.*

Shunryo Suzuki, zen master

At the start of every workshop, I always include a list of housekeeping rules to make the most of our time together. One of the rules I put up is *shoshin*, a word from Zen Buddhism that means 'beginner's mind' – it's also known as 'white belt mentality' in martial arts. It refers to having an attitude of openness, eagerness and lack of preconceptions when studying or approaching a subject, even when studying at an advanced level, just as a beginner would.

The reason I offer this rule to the group is because when we approach things with a beginner's mind, we are more open than we would be if we believed there was nothing to learn or if we thought we already knew it all. In fact, I'd argue that resistance is another form of protection against having to do the real work.

But there's a small chance that, despite everything we've talked about up until now, you think this probably won't work for you as you're either too shy, too timid, too introverted, too reluctant to be in the limelight; that you're too camera/microphone/blog/social media shy, or that you simply have nothing to offer.

What does this have to do with creating an environment where people feel comfortable enough to open up and be their most authentic selves? Maybe you also believe that you have too many skeletons in your closet, or that your stories are way too out there or involve too much drama to share.

I'm here to tell you that it's okay to have all these thoughts and feelings. In fact, as you know by now, these are your defence and protection mechanisms kicking in, trying to keep you safe and comfortable, because you are rattled at the idea of potentially being emotionally exposed. The *Shoshin* environment encourages the lowering of defences.

I'm here to tell you that no matter who you are, no matter how you're built, no matter what's happened in your past or how you feel right now, there is a path for you today to learn how to go from feeling frustrated, overwhelmed or scared to being empowered, excited and inspired to make a difference with your message and story.

# Be the Inspiring Leader You Know You Can Be

When Sarah, a founder and CEO of a successful service-based company, came to me, she knew she was holding back from being more authentic in public. She was a well-respected, sought-after expert in her field and had built a company from scratch that was known for caring and delivering great results for her clients. But when Sarah took to the stage or was invited to talk about herself on various media platforms, she was terrified to talk about her past. So she just skimmed the surface and played it safe, knowing deep down she wasn't being as authentic as she wanted to be.

She knew she had something to offer, something to share. Because she knew deep down that someone out there needed to hear what she had to say, to be inspired and be shown a different way. She knew this was true because she used to be that person who needed to hear how her story unfolded, that there was hope at the end of a dark tunnel.

But she was also her own worst critic. Terrified of what other people might think about her, Sarah kept playing small and pretending as though the version of her that people saw was as good as it got, when deep down she knew she had so much more to offer.

Sharing her story and being more authentic in a professional setting was also the emotional glue that was missing from her impact-driven puzzle. She was going through the motions and although she was very competent and people praised her for her talent and expertise, she knew she was holding herself back. 'If only they knew how much I was panicking inside!' she later told me.

But Sarah was ready to stop hiding behind her business and start daring to be more real in public.

That's when she came to me.

At first she had a lot of resistance to the idea of exploring all the different elements of her life. It always feels uncomfortable to go back in time and open old wounds, stories that involve pain, shame, trauma or feelings we'd rather forget entirely. It's also really hard for us to celebrate our achievements and wins along the way because, as most A-type personalities who are driven by achieving and doing know, it feels scary to slow down, to pause and let it sink in.

But thanks to some convincing, probing and continuous belief in her ability to impact others, she trusted the process. And I kept asking her questions and pausing on moments I felt were significant, asking her to unpack that a little more.

Week in and week out she showed up, willing to share and explore her origin story, open to what might come up. Even if she didn't see the link between what she was sharing or putting down on paper with what her final origin story would be for the public.

For example, when Sarah told me how she felt when she couldn't go on school trips because her mum couldn't afford them, or how people made fun of her because of her poor economic background despite having so much to offer, I knew this would be a crucial part of shaping her story of understanding what it's like to feel unseen or neglected. Which, it turns out, is a huge part of her work today: helping people see their value and be recognised for their great work.

Once we'd mined her life story, we looked at how to shape and share some of her stories that were relevant to the events she had coming up, at first practising in safe environments (with her husband, her close friends and brother) to prepare her to eventually try out some of her stories with slightly higher stakes.

Sarah went from being someone who was terrified of the idea of talking about herself in public, wishing she could be as inspiring as the other people she saw being themselves in public, to being interviewed on a podcast by a major player in her industry where she opened up for the first time about her story.

I'm not going to lie, I was emotional. I smiled wide, knowing how far she had come and how transformational her words would be for her, her business, and the people who needed to hear her courage.

I was full of love and admiration for her. I always am. There is something truly magic about seeing someone come home to who they are and own their story. When we are in the presence of someone who has the courage to let the world know about what they're proud of, what they regret and the lessons they learned along the way from both, especially the difficult ones, we are in the presence of something truly special. Being able to look back at the events that shaped us without any fear of judgement or shame enables us to turn all those experiences into powerful lessons for people to learn from. And to connect with.

The response to her interview was mind-blowing. Her direct messages on social media blew up as more people wanted to reach out and thank her for sharing her story, and more people were interested in finding out more about her work as a result. Her team also felt a new sense of connection with her and the company's mission. She couldn't believe it. If anything, she wished she had started the process you're about to learn a lot sooner.

What I'm about to teach you is the exact same process that I took Sarah through, along with countless other clients. Just like Sarah, you are about to embark on a life-changing transformational journey. Make no mistake about it, if you go through the process and fully commit then you will not be the same person when you're done. No one ever is.

And this process can help anyone. No matter what you think of your story right now, no matter how confused you are about where to start or how all your life stories fit together in one comprehensive piece, trust me. If you stick with the process then you will see the transformational power that sharing your personal story can have.

# Source, Shape, Share: The Authentic Storytelling Framework

The *Authentic Storytelling Framework* will take you from being overwhelmed, confused, scared, scattered and reluctant to share your story to being clear, confident and able to command an audience and get people to care about what you have to say, share or sell. And, more importantly, it will get people to pay attention.

- **Source your story** The first S is *sourcing* all your personal and professional stories. No matter how relevant you may think they are (or not), this is about getting your detective hat on and mapping out all the stories that have shaped you in some way, the highs and the lows. Like a jumbled puzzle, this allows you to make sure that all the pieces are on the floor before you start putting them together in a coherent, impactful and beautiful way to create the picture you want featured on the box. It's the most crucial part of the process.

- **Shape your story** Once you've gathered all the raw material, it's time to learn how to *shape* a story in such a way that people care and pay attention. Forget seven-, nine- or even five-step processes. Shape your story is a *three-step* process that you can apply to any life event to help you carve a memorable, impactful and useful story that will connect with your ideal audience.

- **Share your story** This is where the rubber hits the road, but don't worry: if you're afraid of the idea of *sharing* your story, I've got your back. The biggest issue people face when sharing their story is that they don't have a clear framework or tool that can help them pick and mix the appropriate stories that will have the most impact for their audience. The good news is that you're about to get just that. You're about to learn the power of reverse engineering stories to land your message with your audience. You're going to love this part.

Although the three steps that you're about to take are simple in nature, they do require you to stretch outside your comfort zone and to trust the process. Just like baking the perfect cake, you cannot skip a step, wish things went faster or remove an ingredient.

There's a method to the madness, and this is a linear sequence for a reason. When friends come over for dinner and I cook, I often get compliments on my cooking, but the truth is, I'm not that good at cooking. I'm just really good at following recipes. As you're about to find out, when the process is laid out for you to follow, it's easy to have the impact you want, no matter what you think of your abilities as a public speaker or storyteller (or chef).

This could be the moment you've been waiting for, perhaps for your entire life. The moment where you get an opportunity to embrace all of you. Instead of running away from your truth and being real in public, this is the moment you learn the first steps of running towards it, facing the music and embracing every note it throws at you.

I want you to embrace what it takes to live a more meaningful, purposeful and fulfilling life. And yes, that starts with you. It starts with you committing to the process and to making a promise to your future self, and to the audience you're trying to reach, that you will give this process 100 per cent commitment and withhold any judgement until after the end of the process.

> *The single-frame picture of a caterpillar does not fore-tell its transformation into a butterfly.*[32]
>
> R. Buckminster Fuller

The good news is that this process isn't just about emoting and going deep. It is that, but it can also be a fun process of going from feeling incompetent or overwhelmed to being clear and confident in your ability to impact others with your words.

Too many people go to their graves with their song unsung, but not you. Not on my watch.

This is about acceptance, healing and connection so you may better serve and engage with those who matter the most to you, including yourself.

So kick off your shoes, give yourself a good stretch and let's begin with the first and juiciest step of all:

*Source your story.*

# CHAPTER NINE

# Source Your Story

*Don't let your shame of what other people think run your life.*

Alex Levy, *The Morning Show* (2021)

One of the biggest obstacles people have shared with me about why they haven't fully embraced their origin story is their confusion about which parts of their story actually matter in a business or professional context.

I get it. It's confusing as hell when you're so close to it. I know just how hard it is to see the forest for the trees when you're so close to your own story. When you're standing on top of a mountain it's hard to see just how far you've climbed or how high you are.

But what I've found to be helpful is to surrender the idea of needing to know what's relevant and instead lean into the experience of doing a deep dive into your history to make sure no stones are left unturned.

There's a simple exercise we can do to help you unpack your story and lay it all out in front of you, to help you figure out which elements are helpful (and helpful for others) in better understanding what you're about and why you do what you do.

But first I want to talk to you about my dad's snoring.

## What's Sourcing All About? Piecing Together Clues

As a family, in those rare moments when we were all together and watching TV, my dad would instantly fall asleep. As soon as the show or film started he'd be out cold, mouth open.

But one TV show that always kept him up was *Columbo*, a popular American crime drama starring Peter Falk as Columbo, a homicide detective with the Los Angeles Police Department. In each episode, Columbo would be faced with solving a crime which, from the outset, looked like an impossible mystery to crack. He often appeared as though he wasn't really there, absent-minded, almost dumbing down his intellect. But somehow, at the end, despite how confusing or misleading some of the events may have appeared, and despite the efforts of the culprits to try to scramble the evidence, Columbo would always figure it out. And he always did so in a big reveal where he would map out the story of how the crime took place, who committed it and, more importantly, why he thought they did it. He wasn't so absent-minded after all. In fact, he was always hunting for the clues that would lead him to a clear motive, a *why*, if you like.

More often than not, it was rarely who you thought it was or why you thought it had happened. And my dad would always cheer with delight at how surprised he was at the turn of events, or congratulate himself at having solved the mystery before the big Columbo reveal.

What sticks with me all these years later was that the trick to cracking the enigma was finding the right clues. Columbo had an eye for finding the clues most would have overlooked. He never left any stones unturned and never stopped asking questions. From the outside, his questions often seemed strange, weird, almost simplistic, but I've learned that short, powerful, often dumb-sounding questions are often the most powerful ones you can ask.

Finding your origin story is like detective work. You're constantly trying to find clues, follow a lead, trust an intuition, challenge your assumptions, but instead of looking for a criminal, you're looking for the story, or the element in the story, that makes everything else click together. What you're looking for is what I've come to call the Golden Nuggets. You know them when you find them, but in order to get there it takes a bit of time, patience and the willingness to dig and not shy away from the scary, dark and forbidden places.

It starts with being willing to empty your pockets, no matter how scary that may feel, and put everything on the table. Especially if you have no idea how it all fits together.

## Liam and His Lego

When my brother and I were kids, my parents accumulated bits and pieces of Lego and Duplo – as baby boomers, there's no way in hell they'd waste a single piece. That's how over the years they managed to gather a large collection of stray blocks into a huge denim bag that one of my mum's friends had made, with a red cord to tie it at the top. When it was time to store it away, all you had to do was pull on the red strings to close it up, like Santa's bag. And when you dropped it on the floor it would open up like a mat, spreading all the pieces on the floor, ready to be played with.

I had forgotten about this treasure chest until 2014 when my four-year-old nephew Liam came to stay at my parents' house. My mum asked us to find the bag so that Liam could play with the Lego. As soon as I saw it, I was flooded with memories of my brother and I playing with it and no doubt arguing about who got what pieces (my brother, being four years my senior, probably always won).

We brought the bag into the living room and opened it up. Liam's face was priceless. Beaming from ear to ear, he immediately got cracking, making his way through all the different pieces by first laying them all out on the floor to figure out what he had to play with. He spent hours playing with this set of mismatched pieces, finding countless ways to fit them together to create amazing structures.

When I brought my own kids back to my parents' house years later, Liam and my younger niece Emma were kind enough to get down on the floor and play with them using that same old Lego bag.

**What Liam taught me that day was that in order to see what you're capable of building, you must first make sure that you lay all your pieces in front of you so you know what you have to play with.**

It's exactly the same thing when it comes to unpacking your life story.

If you want to learn how to craft a compelling origin story and build a bank of powerful stories that you can use in different situations then you must first take the time to lay all your stories out.

Like Liam with his Lego, and Columbo with his clues, you must make sure you've got all the information in front of you to see how it all fits together.

And this begins with you taking the time to map out all your professional and personal stories, your Lego blocks of meaningful events that took place in your life.

The key here is to make sure you don't hold back, because holding back in this exercise will only mean that you'll end up with a half-baked story and fall short of having the impact you want.

# How to Source

## PUT EVERYTHING ON THE TABLE

Now is the time to map out your entire life journey: the good and the bad, the highs and the lows, the pretty and the ugly, the successes and the failures; not just the convenient bits, the safe parts, the stories that you've already told before. No, it's time to dive deep and really pull out everything. So if you feel a little uncomfortable right now, that's totally normal. Just remember, you can't cook the perfect dish if you don't know what ingredients you have in your pantry.

In the next paragraph I dive deeper into how to best source your stories, but what I will say now is that one way to go about it is to go back in time and think about all the memorable moments that have shaped your life and start writing them down. They could be memories that bring you joy, or memories that make you sad. The good, the bad and the scary. I personally like to write on a piece of paper or in a notebook I carry around – I'm always prepared.

Keep in mind that memories often come knocking at your door, and if you don't open the door and let them in and get them to sign your guest book (i.e. capture the story), chances are you'll forget them pretty quickly. At least that's what I've found with my process and with my clients', so keep in mind that you will be visited by many memories over the coming days, weeks and months. Your only job is to write them down or capture the essence of them so you can unpack them further when you get a minute. Your job is not to judge them, dismiss them or ignore them. It's just to capture them. It's normal to feel a little overwhelmed at the idea of knowing what stories will be relevant, but the truth is, the only way to figure it out is to first make sure you *have* them. Then you may consciously choose which stories may best serve you, your message and your audience.

In the summer of 2016 I realised I had too much stuff, and so I picked up Marie Kondo's book *The Life-Changing Magic of Tidying Up* and got to work. Kondo's central idea is to remove the clutter in your life by giving away or selling everything that doesn't bring you joy while making sure you only keep the items that do. One of the crucial steps in Kondo's sorting process is to make sure you work your way through your home, not room by room, but rather category by category, meaning that if you want to tackle your books then you should focus on *all* the books in your house, not just the books in your living room. You have to go around your house and collect every book in every room.

The trick is to make sure that you gather everything in one category and lay it all out in front of you, so that you can see all that you have and will no longer be in denial or conflict with reality. It's easy to accumulate things when they're scattered around the house. And take it from me, seeing everything all at once in one place is a wake-up call. My living room floor was covered with over 445 items, from shoes to boxer shorts, back packs to coats. I never imagined that I could accumulate so much stuff. So much so that I made a YouTube video about it that has been viewed over 100,000 times.[33]

When I applied the same process with my story, I realised a couple of things. Number one, I had achieved way more in my life and business than I gave myself credit for, which, to be honest, always feels good. Number two, I realised that I had dismissed too many valuable stories as irrelevant that could absolutely serve my higher purpose to normalise the human condition and make people feel seen, heard and loved. Had I never unpacked everything I never would have been able to see some of the Golden Nuggets I was sitting on.

The point is, you can't evaluate what you have until you see everything you have.

Imagine your life story as a really well-stocked but neglected pantry. You can't know the difference between what's fresh and what's spoiled without handling every single object.

## KEEP DIGGING

It's tempting to do this exercise and remain at a surface level, to play it safe and not go too deep. Maybe you're tempted to just look at your professional achievements or talk about a minor moment in your life that hasn't really had that much of an impact. But the truth is, as you will hear in a moment, this exercise is for you and for your eyes only, so you might as well put on your archaeologist's hat and dig deeply.

My nephew Liam didn't disregard any Lego pieces at first sight. He had to lay everything on the ground so he could take a helicopter view of it all before building his epic castle. Some blocks worked, some didn't, but he knew what he had to work with.

What was amazing was that he could build endless structures using the same set of bricks. By mapping out and sourcing all your stories, you'll create a story bank, or story vault if you want, to draw upon, and you can pick different pieces to share depending on the situation. We'll go over this process in the next chapters.

## FOR YOUR EYES ONLY (IF YOU WANT)

Remember that no one but you has to see what you're about to write down. You're about to go back in time and map out all your anecdotes, stories and events knowing that, if you wish, you will be the only person to see them. You're in control. And that's how you know that you can proceed with complete honesty. Write everything down now, and decide what to share later.

## TAKE CARE OF YOUR NEEDS

Diving into the past can bring up a lot of trapped, unconscious or unprocessed emotions. I always recommend clients seek support during this part of the process, as it can be helpful to know you have someone you can open up to and share with, be it a therapist, an accredited coach or a trusted friend, who can make you feel safe and seen. Make sure to take care of your needs and pull back if it gets to be too much. You can always come back to it later.

## BE AMAZED

When you begin this process you'll revisit memories you had forgotten. Even better, you'll have light-bulb moments of connecting the dots, of seeing the theme or trend that has shaped who you are and why you do what you do.

When you do, let me know, I'd love to hear from you; it's always amazing hearing about light-bulb moments. You can email them to me at Mark@TheUnconventionalists. com, or share them with me by tagging me @markleruste and using the hashtag #glowinthedarkbook on social media (e.g. LinkedIn, Instagram or Twitter). I can't wait.

# Tools for Sourcing

## 1. RIVER OF LIFE

The River of Life is a great tool to help you map out a bank of stories, ensuring you have all the elements you need to craft a compelling story for your ideal audience. It's also a fun and creative way to look back at your life and appreciate what you've achieved, what you've overcome and what you've learned, and to find the stories that best capture chapters of your life that taught you important lessons, things you want to celebrate, achievements, awards, milestones, epic events, but also the heartbreaks, the hardships, the disappointments.

The idea is for you to find two things:

**1.** The two or three *defining events* that have shaped your life (and more than three if you'd like, but I think two to three is good in the beginning) – moments that you can use later on to help paint a picture of who you are.

**2.** We're looking to *connect the dots* of your origin story to clearly crystallise why you do what you do. For most, it's an event from when you were between six and twelve years old. It may not be clear yet how the dots connect, but they do. The connections are there. They always are. I have yet to meet someone who hasn't found them. The connections may not come to you straight away, but trust me, they will.

**What You'll Need**

- Thirty minutes of uninterrupted time

- Paper

- Pen

- Solitude

I personally recommend using a physical piece of paper and a pen instead of your phone or laptop. There's something remarkable about seeing your river of life physically manifested right in front of you, but if you must use something with a screen on it please make sure to print it when you're done.

Set the timer for thirty minutes.

**Set the Scene**

I suggest playing some background music *without lyrics*, as music with lyrics can be distracting. I certainly wouldn't advise listening to a podcast (even mine!) or a TV show while doing this. Studies have found that multitasking is a myth, it simply doesn't work wonders for your attention. Be present in the moment. You'll thank yourself for it later.

You can search online for 'focus music' or 'music for writing'. That's the music I'm listening to right now, as I write this book. My friend Emily Gindlesparger, author of *Please Make Me Love Me*, who is an incredible writer, editor and coach, recommends the Vitamin String Quartet, her favourite no-words focus music. When I asked her for recommendations she added, 'They do string quartet covers of popular music, including things like the entire *In Rainbows* album by Radiohead. It's the perfect balance of something familiar and groovy but not distracting.'

And if you'd rather do this in silence, that's fine too.

---

### Download Your Template

If you like following a clear structure, I've made it easy for you. You can access a free, downloadable and printable template of Your River of Life over at www.GlowInTheDarkBook.com/resources

---

**Get Writing**

On a basic level, your River of Life is an exercise that you will need to write chronologically, like a timeline, from left to right. All the important, memorable, significant or life-changing events that have taken place since you were born, both personally and professionally. As I mentioned, this isn't about knowing what will be relevant to your business or professional goals. This is just 'let's get everything out on the table to see what we've got'. It's about dumping all your story Lego pieces on the floor.

Hold your page horizontally (i.e. landscape).

On the top left-hand side, write the date you were born.

On the bottom right-hand side, write today's date.

You can use the template mentioned previously, or you can draw an S-shaped line that goes across the page, from top left to bottom right, to represent a timeline on to which you can pin events.

That's your timeline for your River of Life.

I like to break it down into blocks of ten years, as a decade is a good manageable chunk to work with. So again, unless you're using the template, you can simply break your S-shaped timeline into chunks of ten years: 0–10, 11–20, 21–30, 31–40, 41–50, etc., so if you're in your thirties, you can have four blocks, or if you're in your forties you can have five blocks.

Although I'll share below some questions that you might find helpful to spark your memory, you can also download a free audio guide where I'll walk you through the exercise using the same questions I use with my clients and participants over at www.GlowInTheDarkBook.com/resources

Write for thirty minutes, no less. You can write longer later, but for now keep it at thirty minutes. Go over every decade of your life mapping out all your professional and personal highs. For example, from birth to your tenth birthday you'll want to think about any vivid memories that come back to you. Maybe it was a family holiday. A birthday party at a friend's house. Or maybe it was something difficult that happened at school. Whatever comes to mind, write it in chronological order (or as close as you can get) in the space allocated to your first decade.

It sounds daunting, but once you get going it's much easier than you think.

### Let's Get Going

I suggest doing this in a few passes. As you go through each decade, start with what you think of off the top of your head. Then, go back again and see what else comes up. Don't hold back, nobody else has to see this apart from you. Some people like to do this all in one sitting, others like to take short breaks or stretch a little between each decade. Don't let yourself get weary or burn out. Fatigue can be fatal to this process, inviting you to take shortcuts. Above all, do whatever feels best for you.

Do a few runs through your timeline and map out your professional and personal highs and lows, but it's important not to judge. This is not the place for that. Even though you may never share a story with anyone, still, put it down.

Think of each story or anecdote as a block of Lego that you're adding to your bag, that you may or may not want to use. But one thing is for sure. If you don't put it in you'll never know if it was the piece you were looking for.

### Prompting Questions

The following list of questions is in no way intended to be a prescriptive list; rather, imagine it being a spark for your fire down memory lane.

## Early Years – Early Teens (Season of Life: Spring)

- What are some of your earliest memories?

- What was it like growing up in your household?

- What was your relationship with your parents like?

- What was great about your family?

- What wasn't so great about your family?

- Any stories that you've been told about when you were a baby? (Were you quiet, easy, difficult, etc.?)

- What were your grandparents like?

- What were your parents like?

- Do you remember your first day at school?

- What was school like?

- Did anything happen to you when you were younger that left a scar?

- What was your favourite summer holiday?

- Who was your best friend?

- Did you have friends at school?

- Do you remember the first time you felt embarrassed? Humiliated? Bullied?

- What is one of your most joyful memories of being young?

- Do you remember the first book you read? The first film you saw? The first CD, song or record you fell in love with?

- What was your earliest memory of money?

- What role did money play in your life?

- Is there anything you saw, witnessed or experienced that was shocking and that you can still remember?

- Did anyone die in your family or close circle of friends?

- Did you start having feelings for other people?

- Did anything happen that should not have happened?

- What else comes up for you?

## Early Teens – Young Adulthood (Season of Life: Summer)

- Where did you grow up?

- What was school like?

- What did you love about school?

- What did you hate about school?

- Who was your first crush?

- Who was your first love?

- Who was the first to break your heart?

- What did you love geeking on?

- What did you and your friends get up to over the weekends?

- Whose heart did you first break?

- What was your first sexual experience like?

- How did you feel in your body as a teenager?

- How comfortable were you with your surroundings?

- What memory comes up when you think about this time of your life?

- Did you go to university?

- Did you drop out of school?

- Was there something someone told you that stuck with you over the years? Maybe a criticism, a compliment or a piece of advice.

- What was your first job?

- Do you remember your first pay cheque?

- What was university like?

- Any stories that took place then?

- How did you end up in your first job?

- What sports were you involved in?

- Did you win any competitions?

- What else comes up for you?

## Adulthood–Parenthood (Season of Life: Autumn)

- Did you enjoy your job? If not, why?

- Did something happen at work?

- How did you end up working in your job?

- Did you get promoted?

- Did you start a business? If so, why?

- What was your lowest moment in your first year of business?

- Who were your mentors?

- Who did you meet that changed the direction of your business?

- What customer feedback made you see things differently?

- What business or career mistakes did you learn the most from?

- Did you stay in a relationship?

- Did someone cheat on you? Or did you cheat on someone?

- Did someone betray you? Or did you betray someone?

- How did you find your partner?

- Did you have kids?

- What was that like? What was great about it? What was tough about it?

- Maybe you wanted to have children but couldn't. How did it make you feel?

- Did you lose a parent? Or a relative?

- Do you remember your first experience of witnessing someone dead?

- What else comes up for you?

## Adulthood–Parenthood (Season of Life: Winter)

- What are you most proud of?

- What did you accomplish that you want to celebrate?

- Where did you hold back and wish you hadn't?

- What are some of the lessons you learned that are dear to you still to this day?

- Who do you want to thank or be grateful for?

- What do you want to leave behind?

- What are you still dreaming of one day doing but still haven't made the time to do so?

- What else comes up for you?

- Is there a day, a moment, an event or a comment where you thought, Fuck this! and decided to pack it all up or walk away from something (or go towards something)?

- What's the most courageous thing you've done?

- Has something happened to you that you never thought you'd recover from but have somehow found a way to do so?

- Another avenue that might help you is to think about the people you've met along the way who made huge differences with seemingly small interventions.

Of course, these are just prompts to help you kickstart your memory. Kickstarting is important: once you stir this memory soup, you'll find that other memories you had totally forgotten about come back. That's great! Just make sure to capture them.

You're looking for pivotal moments that have shaped your life, the key bits that grab your attention. Be sure to look at every aspect of your life – personal, professional, academic, you name it – because you never know where you'll find your life's defining moments.

### Nobody Leaves Lego Pieces in the Corner

When I did this exercise with Robbie Thompson, a peak performance coach who works with CEOs and celebrities and who is built like he could run through a brick wall and come out the other end intact, something came up that he hadn't thought about in a long time. Something he certainly never realised shaped everything he does today as a coach.

He remembered a moment when he was younger and felt physically small and skinny. He picked up a magazine with a muscular athlete on the cover, thinking how cool it would be to look like that, only to remember that there was no way he could. That's when his dad told him: 'You will be like that one day if you want to.' It was something so small, but someone believing in him and telling him that he could achieve something if only he wanted to was a huge moment.

Years later, after a sports injury in sixth form at school, everyone told him he probably wouldn't be able to play rugby again, but a physio told him that not only would he be able to play again, he'd be stronger than ever. And he did and he was.

These two moments that he dug out by doing his River of Life exercise have shaped his entire passion for helping others find a way to reach their optimal fitness. Today, Robbie is that person in your corner. He's the one who sees you as bigger than you see yourself, who holds you to a higher standard than you hold yourself, who believes in you even when you don't. Because he knows what a difference one person or one comment can make to someone's entire life.

Now it's your turn. Go through your River of Life and map out as many life events as you can. Don't hold back. No one will see this. You don't have to share anything that you don't want to, but you still have to get it out on paper.

Remember, nobody leaves Lego pieces in the corner ...

## 2. TIME MACHINE

If you feel stuck, I have an exercise that you might find helpful. Imagine you could get into a time machine and go back to three specific moments in your life to give yourself a word of warning, a piece of advice or just a hug.

When would those moments be? And why?

When I did this exercise myself, I knew exactly where and when I'd go, including the following memory ...

I'm around six years old, sitting nervously behind my desk. My feet can't seem to stop twitching because the air in the space tells me she's about to tell us the very thing I dread to hear the most.

Maybe it's her pacing punctuated by her standing still, or maybe it's because she stares at me a little longer than anyone would be comfortable with.

I know it, I can feel it. She's about to tell us we're in for a treat ...

Because like all world-class sadists, she lives to stretch the tension that comes before the storm.

At this point I'm nervous, fiddling with my pencil, looking outside the window and dreaming of being somewhere, anywhere else but here.

You see, by this point in my short life I had developed coping mechanisms that served me well, including daydreaming while simultaneously glancing at my teacher to pretend I was paying attention.

The trick was to always know the last few words she said so that when she screamed '*Mr Leruuuuuuuuuuste!*' and asked me to repeat what she had just said, I could simply say the last sentence I heard.

*Because God forbid she'd catch me escaping from my pain.*

As I stare at her cold, weathered face and her thick, oversized glasses, I notice that her jet black hair covering her petite but hard face looks like it's been pressed flat into an iron curtain.

I catch myself wondering if that's actually what she does in the morning: wakes up and thinks about how she can terrorise a child today. I bet she had a portrait of Cruella de Vil staring back at her while she performed her evil little morning routine.

She slams her hands together and shouts '*Contrôle surprise!*' – 'Surprise spelling test!' – with a grin so wide the Grinch would feel jealous of being out-grinned.

My heart skips a beat, my palms sweat and the lump in my throat grows bigger, because I know what I'm in for: a public bashing and incoming humiliation.

To me, conjugating a verb or spelling a word is like someone trying to read Japanese or Greek in front of a crowd who happens to not speak either of those languages.

That experience basically sums up a part of my childhood growing up and going to school in France. That feeling of dread I felt every day, at having to face a bully disguised as a figure of authority, was associated with the weighty schoolbooks I hated with all my being, which I had to carry around, skinny as I was.

Because opening up those books when I got home reminded me of how much I hated school and how pointless it all felt. Because those books didn't make me feel more knowledgeable. They made me feel more inadequate.

But what I've come to learn is that the very thing we fear the most is the very thing that has the power to set us free.

Writing books is in no way my favourite way to communicate. It requires too much effort, energy and facing scary demons of my past. I'd much rather speak or talk.

And yet, the book you hold in your hands is published by John Murray Learning, an imprint of Hachette. Hachette happens to also be the publisher of the heavy schoolbooks I once carried around as a child. To see that my book today carries the same logo and knowing that I'm able to share a positive message with others brings me great pride and resolution. Talk about a full-circle story!

Here's the thing: the parts of us that we are most ashamed of, or afraid for the world to see, are actually the very things that make us more human and relatable. The things that feel like they will destroy us make us stronger and more resilient, given enough time, healing and perspective. What I've learned is that wounds can become wisdom with enough time and some perspective.

That's the gift of revisiting some of your earlier memories from the more grounded and adult place of the present.

If I could go back in time and visit my six-year-old self, the young Mark sitting in his classroom feeling stupid, staring at a spelling test he knew he'd fail, scared of the impending humiliation, I'd crouch down next to him, look him in the eyes and tell him that none of this abuse is his fault. That the reason why these teachers are being mean is because they are struggling with their own demons and must be in a lot of pain as well. This doesn't make it okay – it's not okay. None of this should happen. But with time these wounds will heal and all will eventually be well. Despite what my younger self believes, I am smart, kind, creative and will go on to have an amazing life filled with adventures, strong friendships – and one day I will meet the love of my life and start a family of my own. I will go on to raise millions for charity, start my own business and my videos spreading optimism will be viewed by millions of people around the world. One day, no matter how crazy it may sound, I will write books that will make a positive difference in people's lives; and owning and sharing my story, warts and all, will be the birthplace of a healing process for myself and for so many others.

Now it's over to you.

Go through your River of Life using some of the questions above or the time machine exercise, and start mapping out all your memories to create a rich bank of stories. You will use them in the following chapter to help shape the impact you want to achieve.

### What about Doing This with Someone Else?

My advice is to do this on your own first, so that you have an introspective experience of going back in time and doing this in the safety of your own company.

Once you've done that, you can go through the process with a trusted friend or an objective professional who can help you unpack some of your life events. It can be helpful to have someone reflect back to us what they think are the significant events or moments in our life that seem to be relevant to why we do what we do today.

### Need Help?

Talking to someone who doesn't know you can be a really powerful step in finding the narrative in your story, because they're not caught up in all the details and don't know the granular moments of your story. Their brain has to work harder to spot your narrative and to spot your theme. That's why talking to someone who doesn't know you, but who you trust, can be more powerful than talking to someone who knows you quite well. It's certainly more powerful than trying to figure it out for yourself, because you've got too much information and you're too close to it. If you imagine it as a data problem, you've got too much data to spot the trend or theme. You've got to talk to someone who can fish around looking for just the peaks, someone who can zoom out and give you an honest and clear perspective on what you need to see.

If you'd like help in unpacking your story further, you can get in touch with us over at www.theunconventionalists.com or email us at info@theunconventionalists.com. We'd love to help you get some clarity.

## 3. BONUS CHALLENGE: ASK A FRIEND

Ask a friend or a colleague to interview you about your life journey and record it, so you can get it transcribed and be able to pick out some of the bits that are significant to you and to others who hear your story.

What I've found is that it's normal for memories and events to come back to you even after you do this exercise. In fact, your life history is a bottomless well of memories and different methods will help you recall different things, enabling you to access memories that you may have forgotten, so feel free to add them to your River of Life in the days, weeks or months ahead.

I still use the Notes app on my phone to jot down memories when they come to me. I've learned the hard way that if I don't capture them immediately then they often fly away. A lot of the stories I share in this book are from that bank of stories I pulled from my own River of Life.

Again, this is an optional challenge, but you might find it helpful. Either way, by now you will have hopefully dug in and mapped out your River of Life to help you source your story.

# Well Done

Congratulations! You've sourced your story to the best of your ability and now you have a huge amount of stories to pick from. You've left nothing in the Life Pantry and have made sure to dig out everything you could, including all the hidden Lego pieces of your story that were underneath the rug, hidden in a closet or tucked away in a trunk in the attic.

I know what you're probably thinking: Great Mark, now what do I do? I've got all these stories. How on earth am I supposed to make sense of them, let alone know which ones to share or how to share them?

That's because, despite having all the ingredients in front of you, you're still missing the recipe book. But I've got your back. I'm about to teach you an important part of the process, which is how to identify the types of stories in your story bank and understand how to use them.

But for now, well done for having the courage to put it all on paper, and I hope looking at your River of Life enables you to be proud of all the achievements you've had and to celebrate your resilience, strength and courage to have made it through life alive – maybe barely, but alive nevertheless.

In the next part of the process I'll teach you how to map out which stories are which, and turn any anecdote into a powerful story people will remember and connect with.

*Let's dig in!*

# CHAPTER TEN

# Shape Your Story

*I have made this longer than usual because I have not had time to make it shorter.*

Blaise Pascal

## What Is Shaping All About?

If you want to turn a bunch of unrelated and unstructured stories into a remarkable, compelling, vulnerable and impactful personal story, you must learn how to master the skill of shaping and structuring your stories to connect with your audience.

As you know by now, the most valuable thing that you have is the ability to share your stories so that the world listens. How you share your stories, or how you share your origin story, and how well you actually tell that story, matters. A lot.

A well-told origin story is one of the main reasons why inspiring leaders are attracting the right talent, the right partners, the ideal clients and the right opportunities. It's one of the main reasons why people gravitate towards them and want to work with them. An origin story is what made me want to join the Movember Foundation back in 2012. When I first heard Movember's origin story I was attracted to their origin story, mission, vision, values and purpose. I shared more of this back story in my first book, *It's Not You, It's Me: Break Up with Your Job, Make a Difference and Live a Life You Love*.[34] But the skill it takes to share your stories more authentically, and to craft a powerful origin story, starts with the ability to learn how to map out, mould and shape a good story.

The good news about combing through your life and making note of all your professional and personal highs and lows, the defining moments of your life, and the lessons learned along the way, is that you end up with a large pool of stories to play with, which is pivotal to crafting a compelling story down the line.

The bad news is that ... you end up with a large pool of stories to play with. It can be overwhelming, like you're drowning in information. What do you do with all these stories? How do you know which stories matter? Which stories are relevant? For where or when or whom?

Remembering something, no matter how impactful the memory, is very different from being able to share it effectively. The difference between what most people do and what I'm about to teach you is that, on one side, you have people who are just taking up a lot of airtime, making stuff up as they go, with no idea about what message they're trying to convey or land.

On the other, you have those who have taken the time to source their stories, map out the ones that matter most, and have learned how to shape them in such a way that the stories seem effortless when, in fact, they've had a lot of love, time and work poured into them.

**In short, if clarity is key then shaping your story is king.**
Because all great stories, and all great origin stories, start with a simple process of figuring out a way to apply a simple framework to turn any anecdote into a powerful and valuable story.

## Less Is More

Matt, a creative business coach for award-winning agency owners, was struggling to figure out how to share and communicate his stories in a concise, clear and powerful way. He also wanted to be able to share his story on stage without boring his audience or coming across as full of himself.

Like so many founders, Matt struggled from a lack of perspective on what mattered and what didn't. There's a reason why every successful artist has a producer or why every acclaimed director works with a trusted editor. We all need people to tell us what's vital and what can be left out. The creative industry calls it *killing your darlings,* as it can really feel that way when you're being asked to cut out elements that you think are important, when really they're not or, worse, they're distracting from your goal of a meaningful narrative.

When Matt launched into his story the problem was clear. Although he had a great story that made a lot of sense, he was sharing too much information. There was a lot of detail, a lot of different stories and a lot of subplots that went in different directions, confusing his audience and blunting his point.

**Remember, this isn't your Wikipedia page, it's an opportunity to take your audience on a quick, impactful journey.** And to help your audience go from being sceptical about who you are to feeling like they know, like and trust you requires you to take the time to structure your story so that it makes the impact you want.

After going through Matt's story a few times – from feeling unfulfilled pretending to live the life on social media to getting a wake-up call that came in the form of the death of a family friend, forcing him to take a hard look in the mirror, and asking him questions about the different elements of his twists and turns, digging deeper into the uncomfortable moments as well as the moments he was most proud of or had learned from the most – we were able to map out a clear storyline that ran through his story, a narrative thread that he could share no matter the context.

Today, Matt is invited on multiple podcasts and stages to share his story of how on the outside everything looked great but deep down he was miserable, and why he's on a mission to help creative agencies do brave creative work with clients they love.

# How to Shape Your Story

### MAKING SENSE OF YOUR STORY BANK

Before we jump into learning how to shape and structure your stories, I want to make an important point. What you have mined across your River of Life is a collection of stories that carry different meanings and hold different emotional weights for you. Some will be ready and ripe for you to share; others may need a bit more time or professional help to process. And others aren't meant to be shared in a business or professional context. And that's okay.

If going through the River of Life gives you a story bank, then making sure you sort out your stories in the appropriate safe deposit boxes matters. In fact, I've come to learn that the stories in the story bank tend to fall into four categories.

**1. Open-Wound Stories** These are stories we are still in the process of unpacking, processing, making sense of and feeling comfortable enough to share. They carry trauma, shame, grief, wounds, guilt or any other human emotion linked to pain, discomfort or fear of being judged, criticised or rejected when shared. In short, they tend to lean on the heavy shit and stuff that most of us would frankly rather forget or bury so deeply the world would never find out.

Open-wound stories can be the birthplace for potent human connection and provide fertile ground for purpose and direction. Once they're out in the open, they become easier to share. However, some open-wound stories need time to heal before they can be shared, while others you may choose *never* to share. That's okay, and it's entirely up to you. Just know that, when done in a conscious and caring environment, sharing open-wound stories can be extremely therapeutic for both the person sharing them and the people who need to hear them.

**2. Broken-Record Stories** These are stories you've told so many times you've forgotten why they even matter, or how to give them emotional resonance. You're tired of telling your broken-record story, but, like a classic golden oldie, you just keep telling it because you know it so well.

The problem with broken-record stories is that while they're comforting they're also dangerous because we're bored with them. And people can feel that when they hear them. The good news is that, with a little work and awareness, you can turn these stories around.

3. **Interesting but Irrelevant Stories** These may be fascinating to you and have shaped you in some way, but they're not relevant or interesting to anyone else. You'll learn how to sift these out in the next chapter, but for now just know that you may fall into the trap of thinking a story is brilliant when it's not.

4. **Impact-Driven Stories** These are the secret sauce to any great leader, the stories that people pay attention to, remember and want to share with others; stories where the structure is well thought out, the flow is seamless and the point is clear and useful. They are the stories that have been carefully curated and crafted, fine-tuned and highly intentional at their core.

Impact-driven stories feel natural, almost spontaneous, and help connect the dots, but have been workshopped behind the scenes to serve a specific purpose. Think of them as finely tuned emotional guided gift missiles aimed at the heart. They're usually just outside our comfort zone but are ripe for the picking in the right context and situation, and with the right amount of prep work. In short, they are the stories we all want to hear and connect with.

A little care and attention can turn any of the first three story types – open-wound, broken-record and interesting but irrelevant – into an impact-driven story. And the way to do that is to apply the *Impact-driven Storytelling Formula* that you're about to learn.

## One Framework to Rule Them All

Most story-building techniques, from Aristotle to Joseph Campbell, are great in theory, and can deliver amazing results, but for most of us who have a business to run and customers to serve, they can be daunting and hard to implement because they aren't designed with *business* in mind. That's why I fine-tuned a simple, three-step formula that simplifies the process with an eye toward impact-driven stories.

## The Three Golden Rules of Impact-Driven Stories

As you begin to shape your story, do so with this end in mind: you are looking to craft a story that will be *clear*, that will *connect*, and that will be *considerate* of your future audience.

1. **Clarity** Know what you need to say, why it matters, and how to share enough of your story for your audience to understand what's going on but not so much that they switch off or check out midway through.

2. **Connection** Connect with your audience by sharing not just the good bits about your story but also the bits that were challenging or that you'd rather forget. Audiences root for people who are willing to show up and own their

shortcomings, who turn difficult situations into powerful lessons. If you want people to talk about your story long after you've stopped talking, make sure you connect with them on an emotional level.

**3. Consideration** Consider your story with your audience in mind. Does it include worthwhile takeaways? Will they learn lessons or acquire knowledge that they can apply later? Remember that while it's important to tell stories that will hold your audience's attention, it's just as important to tell stories that provide practical value. Doing less than that is disrespectful to your audience. They expect value from you; you have to deliver. Respect your audience by doing so.

# What Is a Story?

**Storytelling is actually quite simple.**

As Donald Miller says in his book *A Million Miles in a Thousand Years: What I Learned While Editing My Life*, 'A story is a character who wants something and overcomes conflict to get it.'

That's it.

If you can remember that and understand that then you pretty much understand everything you need to know about storytelling and what we need to hear in a story to feel engaged by what you say and share. Everything else is bells and whistles.

That's the beauty of sharing your story. It can be clear and simple, and when it comes to storytelling, clear and simple wins.

## THE IMPACT-DRIVEN STORYTELLING FORMULA

There are many storytelling formulas, from the five Ws of journalism to the three-act structure to Joseph Campbell's 12 Stages, but none of them is optimised for turning your life events into impactful stories. That's where the Impact-driven Storytelling Formula comes in.

Go through your River of Life stories and pick one that you think has the potential to be an impactful story, one that tells a story of overcoming hardship, succeeding in spite of the odds, persevering through difficulties, and that has the potential to teach a lesson and connect emotionally to an audience. Don't tell me you don't have one: I know that you do!

Now, grab a pen and paper and evaluate your story in the light of the following three steps.

### 1. Context (Tell Me)

The *context* part of the formula sets the scene. It gets us into the story quickly by telling us *where, when* or *what* we need to know to set it up. Draw us a picture. For example:

> *In 2016, four weeks after I quit my job to start my own business with all the hopes and dreams that come with a newly found venture, I found myself sitting on the floor in the middle of the afternoon in my small flat, sobbing uncontrollably …*

Just set the scene. Give us enough information (but not too much) to know where you are, what's going on, maybe how old you are or what year it is, but we don't need all the details. Just enough to keep us from wondering, Wait, when was this? or Wait, where was this? What was going on? If your audience worries about basic information, they might miss the real point of your story. In short, if your audience are too busy thinking, they're not connecting with what you're saying.

How will you set the scene in *your* story? Figure it out and write it down.

Once you've established the context it's time to connect with your audience by sharing your story's emotionally charged moment.

## 2. Connection (Take Me)

The second step, *connection*, brings us into the story and connects us emotionally to what you were experiencing at the time. It's a deeper level than just the facts. It enables your audience to feel an emotion and pay more attention to what you're about to say.

Continuing from above:

*Staring at my bank account balance, I realised I didn't know how I was going to pay my mortgage that month. I had somehow run out of money as I was too busy focusing on creating content and posting on social media instead of generating sales. I was in tears. I was ashamed. This was not how I had imagined my life, and my business, would turn out. I felt as though I couldn't tell anyone as I was just so embarrassed.*

Make it real, grab your audience's attention by sharing something that you really felt in the moment or that can help them really *feel* something. Not too much, though. Like salt and pepper, overdoing it leaves a sour taste in the mouth. Plus you're not sharing a story for the sake of fishing for tears or for people to feel sorry for you. You're telling a story to make a point.

How will you make an emotional connection in your story? Write it down.

Now that you've brought your audience into your story and opened up about something real, it's time to make it actually useful for your audience. It's time to draw out the lesson your story is meant to convey.

### 3. Conclusion (Teach Me)

*Conclusion* is about sharing the universal lesson, message or key takeaway your story carries. What is the key point? Even though it may be obvious to you, the key is to make it clear to everyone else.

What's in it for the audience? The point you want to land is what makes your story relevant and not just an entertaining anecdote.

If you're struggling to work out what the universal truth is in your story or what key message you can draw from your story for your audience, think about what this experience, event or moment taught you. If you were bullied, how did you overcome it? If you went bankrupt, how did you recover? If you got fired, how did you rise above it? The ultimate power of your story isn't in the pain, it's in the recovery. The harder the lesson was for you, the more you can help others.

No matter what the story is, there are always one or more lessons you can draw out of that experience that other people would find valuable.

Continuing on:

*That's when I realised that what I had wasn't a business but an expensive hobby. Instead of generating more leads and conducting more sales conversations to get more clients for my business, I had spent all my time posting on social media, creating great content. In short, I had failed to focus on the basics of business. What I realised was that, too often, we like to focus on the things that are fun and sexy, but burying our head in the sand over the things we know we need to do (but ignore) is never a good long-term strategy. What I realised was that I needed to focus on what mattered, not what felt exciting.*

What's the underlying point of your story, the lesson that your audience can take home with them and apply tomorrow at work? Remember, the best lessons are sometimes embarrassing to the storyteller. Got it? Good. Write it down.

You may not be aware of this formula, but chances are you've seen many people use it when sharing stories about their life, how they started their business, why they launched this product or service and, more importantly, celebrating their customer's success story.

The reason I'm often able to spontaneously pull stories out of thin air isn't because I'm a natural-born storyteller. It's because I've internalised this formula and I can instantly put any story through that process and turn it into something valuable. Practise the three steps of context, connection and conclusion, and you'll be able to do it too.

## How It Looks on the Other Side

Mike Michalowicz is the author of six books, including *Profit First* (2014), *Fix This Next* (2020), *The Pumpkin Plan* (2012) and *Clockwork* (2018). Mike often shares his origin story of why he ended up changing his life and focusing his purpose on eradicating entrepreneurial poverty. Here's how he often talks about it:

> It was 14 February 2008, Valentine's Day, when I got a call in the middle of the afternoon from my accountant. He said I needed to declare bankruptcy. (Context)
>
> I went from being a self-made millionaire to not being able to afford a twenty-dollar horse-riding lesson for my daughter. (Connection)
>
> My nine-year-old daughter ran upstairs and offered her piggy bank savings to support the family after I told them we were broke. As tears came rolling down my face, that's when I knew I had to stop hiding my head in the sand and become financially savvy to never have to put my family through this again.[35] (Conclusion)

See how Mike uses the formula to turn a difficult memory into a powerful story that audiences can share and remember?

# Get Writing

Now that you've learned the Impact-Driven Storytelling Formula, identify the concepts of context, connection and conclusion in the River of Life memory that you picked earlier and put it all together into a powerful, emotional, impactful story.

You might end up with a pretty long document in which you've added a bunch of details and weaved in information just to make sure we 'get it'. Now your challenge is to make it fit on one side of an A4 sheet (standard copy paper in the US). This means you'll have to learn how to cut it down, trim down some of the information and keep it lean. Remove everything that isn't essential to context, connection and conclusion. Remember, less is more.

Then cut it some more.

Now that you've got it on a single piece of paper, it's time to cut it down to half a page. Keep winnowing down until there is no fat left to trim. The more you repeat this process, the clearer and more impactful your story will be.

# Congratulations! Now Do It Again

Well done! You've taken a memory you dug out of your River of Life, applied a simple three-step formula, and turned it into a short, powerful, impactful story that can improve the lives and businesses of people around the world.

Maybe you picked a story to explain why you do what you do, or maybe you picked a story to explain the origin story of your business. Either way, now pick three or four more memories from your River of Life and do it all over again. The more you do it, the quicker the exercise will become, and the better your end results will be. After you've done several of these, go back and look at your first one again. With the expertise you've gained you'll almost certainly see ways to improve it.

Keep this up and you'll build a bank of personal stories that you can pull out of your bag and share at any given moment. Above all, you should be able to weave a few of them together to make a longer, cohesive narrative that tells the story of who you are and how you reached your destination, the events that changed you and shaped you. We'll cover how to map out your origin story in a moment, but for now, celebrate the fact that you have the ability to apply a practical filter to turn any of your life events into a powerful, memorable and impactful story!

# The Impact-Driven Storytelling Formula in the Wild

All great entrepreneurs and business leaders need to have a powerful story to tell about their lives, their businesses, their products or services, and their customers. The same technique we just used for your River of Life stories can be applied to any other type of story. Why did you start your company? Why did you launch your core product? How has your business transformed lives? How have you amazed (and disappointed) your customers? The possibilities are endless.

Here are a few examples of founders and entrepreneurs who use the power of storytelling to connect with their audience and make people care about what *they* care about. I've applied the Impact-Driven Storytelling Formula to each one.

---

**Nir Eyal, author of *Hooked: How to Build Habit-Forming Products* (2013) and *Indistractable: How to Control Your Attention and Choose Your Life* (2019) (Personal Story)**

*I grew up in central Florida where football was a really big deal, in fact it was pretty much God, football and everything else. Although our high-school's football coach could pretty much do whatever he wanted, my public school didn't have enough teachers, so they asked him to teach this one class. And that one class was a class I was in. But all we did was read* Time *magazine!* (Context)

*But I found something special inside what was, at the time, a very big deal of a magazine. You see, I grew up in a very conservative part of central Florida, I had this really weird name, there was maybe one other Jew in my school, let alone anybody from Israel or with a strange-sounding name. And I'm actually dyslexic, so I was always a really slow reader. Plus I was overweight. I really felt like an outsider.* (Connection)

*But my favourite part around reading Time magazine in class was the last page, which always contained an op-ed. These essays were phenomenal. I remember reading these articles with the class and then discussing them and seeing people's minds change and expand. And through that discussion facilitated by these articles people who were set in their ways would sometimes take a different viewpoint. I just thought that was incredible. That's when I really fell in love with persuasive essays and saw how writing could change the way we think about and see each other, and the world.* (Conclusion)

You can imagine young Nir struggling to fit in, feeling like an outsider and not confident in his ability to read, falling in love with the articles he was reading and the powerful discussions they triggered in his classroom, and discovering how a piece of writing could bring people together and change people's minds. No wonder he became a professional writer!

## Billie Quinlan, co-founder of Ferly (Business Story)

*Back in 2017 I joined Zinc, a six-month business accelerator programme based out of London. As part of the programme, a mix of experts and academics came in to talk to us about the different pillars of women's wellbeing and mental health, including bipolar, schizophrenia and pregnancy.* (Context)

*But the crazy thing is, not a single person came in to talk to us about sexuality and the role sexuality plays in our health and quality of life. The reason why my co-founder Anna and I were so aware that this wasn't even on their radar was that Anna lost her virginity when she was raped at fifteen and I was sexually assaulted at work in 2016.* (Connection)

*Even in a programme that was dedicated to women, they still didn't feel comfortable talking about sex. So we decided we were going to talk about it. That's why Ferly exists, to radically transform women's relationship with sex.* (Conclusion)

In a few short paragraphs Billie shares a powerful reason for founding a company to tackle issues that affect millions of women but felt like no one else had the courage to even discuss.

## Josh Bolding, Co-founder of Vivo Life (Product Story)

*When we created Vivo Life, we never set off with the intention of creating a multivitamin, as we wanted to focus on creating the best natural protein powder in the world. But we kept getting emails from our customers requesting we look into it.* (Context)

*The more we looked into it, the more we realised how many synthetic multivitamin pills were packed with fillers, binders and artificial ingredients that just weren't good for you. That's when we realised we couldn't just stand by and do nothing, we had to somehow find a way to take on the multivitamins industry.* (Connection)

*It took us over five years to formulate THRIVE, and it's been backed by over fifty independent studies. THRIVE is a truly revolutionary health supplement that has all the power of a multivitamin but is made with 100 per cent natural ingredients like spinach, kale and baobab fruit. Each scoop has the antioxidant equivalent of ten servings of fruits and vegetables along with fifteen essential vitamins and minerals, including vitamin B12, vitamin D, iron and zinc. The response from our community has been unbelievable. No one should have to compromise between optimal supplements and natural ingredients that are good for you and the planet.* (Conclusion)

As you can tell, this simple yet powerful formula can be used to craft and create multiple stories that you can share about yourself, your product and your business. It can also help craft a story about your customers.

## Scott Harrison, Founder of charity: water (Customer Story)

*Instead of asking for gifts on her ninth birthday in June 2011, Rachel Beckwith asked for donations to help bring clean water to those who had none. Her goal was to raise $300 to build wells in Africa.* (Context)

*She fell $80 short and pledged to try again when she turned ten. Five weeks later, after making her pledge, Rachel died from injuries she sustained in a road accident. Her friends and family took up her cause and reignited her campaign. Her story went viral, inspiring donations from across the globe. Within months, they had far surpassed Rachel's original goal and raised more than $1.2 million.* (Connection)

*Her original birthday campaign funded 143 water projects, helping to bring clean water to more than 37,770 people in Ethiopia. Rachel's story reminded me just how much of an impact one life really can have.* (Conclusion)

# Next Steps

Now that you've started to play with and apply the three-step Impact-driven Storytelling Formula, hopefully you can see how to take a story – *any* story – out of your story bank and turn it into something much more than just a nice anecdote.

Knowing how to source and shape your story is good, but if you really want to have the impact you desire, you also must learn how to share it.

In the next chapter we're going to demystify one of the most important parts of the process: how to know and choose the most appropriate stories depending on the context in which we find ourselves and the audience we find ourselves speaking to.

It's one of the most exciting parts because this is where you get to see the impact your stories can have on the world.

*I can't wait.*

# CHAPTER ELEVEN

# Mapping Your Origin Story

**How do I know which stories I should use from my River of Life to create my origin story?**

Now that you've mapped out some of the significant events that have shaped your life, you probably have one question: Great, Mark, but how do I know what stories to pick, and how do I make it all make sense? How do I pick a series of events from my list of stories and weave them together or pick a singular event and map it out to shape my origin story?

I'm so glad you asked.

What I've found is that people tend to come across three main issues in the process of mapping their origin stories in a clear, compelling, short and punchy way:

**1.** They over-complicate it by either adding too many details or opening up too many story loops, as though they have to give the entire back story of their life (including what time and what day of the week they were born) in order to establish the context. Trust me, you don't. Less is more.

**2.** They can't find any logical or emotional explanation as to why they do what they do, as though they just accidentally wound up where they are and whatever happened to them in their formative years has nothing to do with what or why they do what they do today. This could be resistance to linking an event to the reason for your passion, or it may mean you need help to find the common thread that will lead you to connecting the dots. Regardless, the dots always connect, it's just a matter of figuring it out.

**3.** They try to crowbar all their life experiences into one narrative, but it feels too forced or unclear for your audience to grasp. As tempting as it may be, the point here isn't to let the world know of all the wonderful things you've done or all the hard lessons you've learned. Instead, it's to focus on the prize: help your people make sense of why you do what you do so they can be affected by it and go on to share your story like wildfire.

What you're aiming for when you are sharing your origin story is to convey empathy and credibility.

That's why the key thing here is to be open to exploring what some of your life events may have in common or finding out how they may be linked to what you do today. It may not be clear to you now, but when you dig a little deeper, when you unpack your experiences a little more, then events that seemed banal or mundane suddenly become the foundational myths of your origin story, i.e. the *pièce de résistance* of why you do what you do.

Take Malcolm for example.

# Malcolm and the Magical Mouse

When I asked Malcolm, the CEO of a creative agency, to volunteer to share some of his early childhood memories, he shared the story of when his dad, who was a professional photographer, took him into his studio for the very first time.

Malcolm was around eight years old and he remembers walking around this buzzing creative place, with people doing all sorts of fun-looking activities, while his dad described the different roles people played in a creative studio.

At one point, as he was introducing himself to his dad's colleagues, he came across something he'd never seen before: a large silver screen, displaying some amazing graphics, mounted on a desk. But what caught his eye was the little object the graphic designer was moving around.

'It's pretty neat, huh?' she said. 'It's called a "mouse". It helps me navigate around my screen so I can click on things and helps me do my work faster and better.'

Malcolm was in awe. This was the first time he had seen a mouse with an iMac and he thought it was the most beautiful thing he'd ever seen.

As he recalled this memory, I asked Malcolm to describe how it made him feel; what it opened up for him.

*'Walking around my dad's studio made me realise that you can do creative work and get paid. People seemed to be having such a good time. But what I remember the most is the way I felt when I saw that first Apple mouse, it was just incredible. That feeling of seeing something both beautiful and functional just blew my mind. I still remember it today.'*

Interestingly, Malcolm helps clients with their visual identity and overall branding, and as we unpacked his story a little further, what I helped Malcolm to realise was that what he wants to do is help his clients achieve that same first impression with their branding, be it logos or their website, that he got when he saw that first mouse on his dad's colleague's desk – that wow factor that takes your breath away and creates an emotional bond that stays with you forever.

You could have seen a light bulb switch on in Malcolm's eyes as he connected the two. 'Oh my God! I never realised, but that's exactly it!'

In that moment, Malcolm went to work and started crafting a short origin story.

The simple yet powerful story he'd been sitting on for over three decades, waiting to be fully unleashed, was finally out in the open. It helped Malcolm feel more confident in his ability to engage prospective clients and inspire his audiences, especially when he introduced himself and shared why he started his company.

# The Magic Formula

When I was invited to give my TEDx talk at TEDxCardiff in 2017 I talked to as many TEDx organisers and TEDx speakers as I could, to ask them about what they thought worked and what didn't. I read as many books, watched as many videos and read as many articles as I could on public speaking and what makes an impactful TED-like talk.

One thing that kept coming up was the importance of having a central idea that you want to share. Not two, three or five different ideas. No, just one clear, compelling idea that you want to share.

And in order to make that happen, you need an idea, an idea that's simple enough to fit on the back of a napkin.

Here are a few examples of simple central ideas:

- The central idea of Brené Brown's TED talk, 'The Power of Vulnerability', is that, unlike what we've been led to believe, 'vulnerability is not weakness; it's our greatest measure of courage'.

- In his powerful TED talk 'We Need to Talk About an Injustice', Bryan Stevenson points out that in the US, the justice system 'treats you much better if you're rich and guilty than if you're poor and innocent'. You could also argue that his central idea is similar to a quote attributed to Martin Luther King Jr: 'The arc of the moral universe is long, but it bends toward justice.'

- The late Sir Ken Robinson's TED talk 'Do Schools Kill Creativity?', the most watched TED talk of all time, captures his central idea that education stifles creativity because schools don't embrace and celebrate failure.

- When Steve Jobs gave his 2005 Stanford Commencement Address, the message that stayed with me, and with so many others, was 'Stay hungry, stay foolish'.

As I watched my favourite talks, I picked out the central idea that stood out and made me pay attention. I recommend you watch some TED talks or famous talks given by people who made an impact, and do the same. It'll help you see your own stories in a new light.

Although defining a central idea is one of the hardest things to do, as it turns out, keeping things short and simple is also notoriously hard; and it cannot survive without the next vital element of any great story: information that supports your consistent plot line.

# It Takes Years to Become an Overnight Success

In 2009 Simon Sinek stepped on stage at TEDxPugetSound to give his talk 'How Great Leaders Inspire Action'. Better known as 'Start with Why', his talk quickly became the second most watched talk on TED.com.

Sinek's central idea is that 'people don't buy WHAT you do; they buy WHY you do it'. Every example, story, stat, fact, question, quote and anecdote that he shares supports and illustrates this central core idea.

What people may not realise is that Simon Sinek had given that talk hundreds, if not thousands, of times before stepping on stage at TEDx. He had run workshops on the same topic for years, so he knew his point and the arguments he needed to make to land it.

I'm sure Simon had more stories and examples to share (as he usually had hours-long workshops to convey his point), but he knew they were a distraction to his main point. By going through the gruelling process of eliminating anything that didn't support his argument, of cutting out anything that distracted the attention and focus of his audience from the point he was trying to make, he transformed an hours-long workshop into an eighteen-minute talk that has impacted over 57 million people and counting.

# Reverse Engineering

Reverse engineer your story – start with where you are now and work backwards – to make sure that the stories you choose to share are in line with what you do today. Think of it like a lawyer trying to build a case and having to convince a jury. She knows where she wants the jury to be; now she has to build a clear narrative that showcases irrefutable arguments to prove her point. She has to process all the information and sift through truck loads of data to clarify and simplify the narrative she has to present to the jury.

Your origin story demands exactly the same process. You know where you are. You know the idea you want to communicate to your audience. You have a bag filled with ideas from your River of Life. Now work backwards from your present status and the message you want to convey and figure out which episodes of your life support your goals. Hand-pick specific events that support why you do what you do and disregard everything else for the sake of clarity.

It doesn't mean that all your other life events don't matter, they do. In fact, you'll need them in your back pocket to bring out when asked specific questions about your past, but when it comes to your origin story, your job is to make it easy for people to connect the dots and see why what you do matters.

# Exercise

Now that you know the secret formula to map out a draft version of your origin story, reverse engineer yours by going through your River of Life to pick out an event or a series of events that you can weave together while staying on point, focusing on examples that illustrate why you do what you do today.

Then try it out on people and see if it makes sense to them. Ask yourself these questions: Are you using too many stories? Are you giving too much detail? The idea is to introduce yourself, explain why you do what you do, and establish your credibility, authority and empathy as quickly as possible.

A well-crafted and curated origin story does just that.

# CHAPTER TWELVE

# Share Your Story

## Jesus and the Parrot

When I was around eight years old, my mum told us that she had managed to get tickets to attend the live prerecording of *The Jonathan Ross Show* that was taking place at the Videopolis Theatre in Disneyland Paris.

We took our seats in the massive theatre. Hundreds of people were in attendance. There was a great buzz and it was amazing to be behind the scenes of such a production, with people running around with clipboards and microphones, using walkie-talkies to pass on codes for dimming the lights or cueing up the music.

When Jonathan Ross came on stage everyone cheered and clapped. Between the shots of him talking to the camera or repeating a sequence or talking to guests, including Diana Ross (the former lead singer of the vocal group The Supremes), there were people trying to keep the audience entertained, amused and in high spirits.

This included a series of activities, one of which was an opportunity for volunteers in the audience to share their favourite joke.

I raised my hand as high as my tiny eight-year-old frame would allow and, to my surprise, I was picked. One by one, the other kids shared their jokes while I tried to figure out which joke I was going to tell.

Their jokes were short, sweet and appropriately innocent. By the time the microphone came to me, I launched myself into a joke I knew had worked pretty well in the courtyard with my friends that week:

*A parrot walks into a bar and asks the barman for a Coca-Cola. To which the barman takes offence and says he doesn't serve Coca-Cola. The parrot insists, but the barman won't budge.*

*This goes on for a while until the barman tells the parrot he's had enough: 'Listen, if you don't stop going on about your bloody Coca-Cola I'm going to pin you to the wall, you hear me?'*

*To which the parrot replies, 'I want a Coca-Cola!'*

*The barman grabs the parrot, walks across the room and pins the parrot's wings to the wall with nails. As the parrot looks around, he notices Jesus on the cross, and says, 'Did you ask for a Coca-Cola too?'*

Now I can still remember saying that joke and thinking it was hilarious, but instead of hysterical laugh I was met with the hostess snatching the microphone from my hands and only a smattering of nervous laughter from the crowd.

I didn't quite get the reaction, considering I knew the joke had worked well before. Maybe people didn't appreciate me talking about animal cruelty? Or were people sensitive about jokes involving Jesus? I was confused.

The hostess thanked us all but before letting us go back to our seat, she leaned in and whispered in my ear, 'Don't ever say that joke again.'

My mum, who as a Christian must have thought she'd raised me better, was mortified that her son had made a Jesus joke in front of a live TV audience attending *The Jonathan Ross Show*, but what I learned in that moment was the same joke that worked a treat with my friends in the courtyard at school wasn't appropriate in this context.

When it comes to sharing stories, context matters. So does knowing your crowd.

As you will learn shortly, our stories need to have a certain degree of risk – risky enough to forge connection on a deep level, but appropriate enough to not push others too far and risk disconnecting altogether. Being agile with your intended and unintended impact is a skill you can and will master as you start sharing your stories.

# Sharing Is Daring

There's an art and a skill to picking appropriate stories for a context and setting. It's something that those who've fallen short of their storytelling goals and dreams have often failed to master.

Lucky for you, I've developed a technique that will help you to

- create the intended impact

- feel safe knowing you're in control

- be ready and excited to share your story

# How It Works

When Daniel Priestley kicks off the first day of his 'Key Person of Influence' business accelerator, he shares well-selected stories that help to set the scene. If you hear him deliver a keynote presentation, you'll also hear him sharing the same stories that highlight key messages he wants the audience to connect with.

One of them goes something like this. When Dan was around nine years old, he came home to find that half his house had burned down. Instead of throwing away all the household items, he managed to salvage a few and organised a garage sale.

As he was proudly displaying his 'inventory', a man came by to take a closer look. It was the toaster that grabbed his attention. He asked how much it was. Daniel said, 'Twelve dollars.'

The man asked Dan's dad if he was willing to negotiate the price. Dan's dad said, 'You're talking to the wrong guy. He's in charge.'

That was the moment Dan got the entrepreneurial bug because he felt amazing knowing he was in charge and could be in control of something that could generate an income.

If you hang around Dan long enough you'll also hear a few of his other flagship stories, including the one about how he and his buddies organised student disco nights for other students by partnering up with nightclubs and getting sponsors involved. Or how he climbed a mountain in Bali in the early morning to watch the sun rise, only to realise he was so focused on looking at all the other mountains as his guide pointed them out that he had forgotten to appreciate the mountain he was on.

What you might not realise is that Dan picks stories from his story bank with purpose and intention. He knows that depending on what message he's trying to convey, who he's talking to and where he's delivering his story, he will pick the appropriate story to do it the best justice.

What I've learned over the years is that the power to have the impact you want, and make people care about what you have to say, is in reverse engineering your stories according to the context, audience, your message and platform on which you find yourself.

Take Dan's example. If Dan wants to convince an audience about the importance of partnership, he could share the story about him and his friends organising student nights and making a hefty profit thanks to the partnerships he made with the nightclubs. If he wants to convey why he fell in love with entrepreneurship, you can be sure he'd tell the story about his garage sale.

However, if Dan wants to convince you that you're standing on a mountain of value but you don't even know it because you're simply too close to it, he will pull out his story about climbing the mountain in Bali.

You, too, can learn how to craft the appropriate story based on the message or point you're trying to land, and with whom and where you're sharing it.

Let's break it down.

## Context

The *context* determines what is appropriate for you to share.

Are you sitting across from a therapist? Or are you standing across from a potential investor? Are you being interviewed on a HARDtalk-style prime-time television show? Or are you being invited on a long-format interview podcast known for being honest and real? Are you speaking on a stage that is being streamed live to thousands of people online? Or are you speaking to a small classroom of students behind closed doors?

Knowing the context in advance is critical to picking and choosing the most appropriate stories to share. If you want to become a master at reverse engineering the right stories for the right moment, it begins with understanding the context, because that's what determines what type of story is most appropriate and what you feel most comfortable sharing.

For example, as mentioned previously, picking from your open-wound story basket may feel more comfortable and safe in the context of being with a therapist, a professional or a friend you trust intimately.

When my mum opened up to my dad for the first time in her early twenties – after leaving her country and moving in with him in a tiny flat outside of Paris – about the truth of her family dynamic and the secrets she had felt so much shame about, she was met with acceptance, empathy and a combination of words that would forever change her relationship to herself and to her story: 'It's not your fault. None of this is. It's a disgrace you were used as a scapegoat. No matter what you've been told, this is not your fault.' Up until that moment she had always believed she was the one to blame, that she was responsible for what had happened. As that's what she had been told her whole life. As a result, she was sure that people would judge her, reject her. So she had kept this secret to herself for almost two decades. And yet here she was, living in a new country, opening up to a man for the first time despite having known him as a friend for years. When my mum recounted this story to me, I was moved to tears. The idea of my mum having to carry around the weight of guilt and shame for two decades because of what she thought would happen if she opened up crushed my heart. And yet I'm so glad she had the courage to share with my dad, a man who she felt safe enough to open up to. In that moment she realised that everything she was led to believe wasn't true, and she could start to let go of the guilt, shame and trauma.

Within context I would also include topic.

Topic is simply knowing ahead of time what the overall topic or agenda for the conversation, talk or interview will be. When I get asked for an interview on a podcast I always ask for the podcast's theme or topic. If I'm speaking on a podcast that covers modern leadership I'll choose different stories than if I'm talking on a podcast about how to become a public speaker.

Same platform, but different context and topic.

Once you understand the context, it's time to understand the platform.

# Platform

The *platform* is the medium in which you'll be sharing your story.

Are you a guest on a podcast? Are you being asked a question on a panel in front of a live audience? Are you speaking one-on-one with a potential client over the phone? Are you being interviewed by the press? Are you speaking at a virtual event? You get the picture. The platform gives you an idea of what is appropriate in terms of length of your story and what kind of story to share.

If you're invited on a long-format podcast then you know you'll have a longer time to unpack and share your story.

A podcast is also less of a visual medium, so you may be more relaxed than if you have a camera pointed at you.

On the other hand, if you're introducing yourself on a panel or are posting on social media then the platform will mean you have a shorter amount of time and therefore will have to convey your point much more quickly.

That's why I would also add time within platform.

Time is simply knowing how long you have to introduce yourself and share your stories. A long-format podcast will be a lot more forgiving than a live TV interview where you have a minimum amount of time to convey your message. Knowing the platform and the context will help you determine time, so you will be able to see ahead of schedule how much time you have.

Of course there are a ton of platforms where you could find yourself sharing your story, but here are a few examples to get you started:

- On your website

- On a podcast

- On stage

- With your team

- In a pitch

- On a sales call

- On a live or virtual panel

- With a potential partner

- With a client

- In marketing material

- In your book

- In the media

- On social media

- At a school

- In a workshop

The platform, along with the content, will give you another crucial element to having an impact with your story and picking and crafting the right message. The next one is knowing your audience.

# Audience

Although LinkedIn and Instagram are both social media platforms, they represent two different types of *audience*, the same way that *The Wall Street Journal* or *The Sun* have different audiences.

Speaking at a public event to a group of strangers or speaking at your private all-staff annual event changes who you're speaking to and what you should say.

Determining who your audience is enables you to craft the appropriate stories to introduce yourself in a much more compelling way. For example, if you're speaking at a school about your journey, how you overcame obstacles and achieved what you have, you'll probably use different language and stories to illustrate your points than you would if you were in a stand-up comedy club speaking to a boozy crowd.

Lastly, reverse engineer your story to ensure maximum effect by asking yourself three questions:

- What do I want this audience to *feel* at the end of my story?

- What do I want this audience to *think* at the end of my story?

- What do I want this audience to *do* at the end of my story?

Think about how you can present your story so that it accomplishes these three goals.

## Message

You'd be surprised by how few people actually take the time to think about what *message* they want to share, or what the intention of sharing their story will be.

For example, depending on who I'm speaking to, I would use a different conclusion to my story of being bullied by schoolteachers. If I'm speaking to founders and entrepreneurs, I would finish by landing that I know what it feels like to not have a voice. If I'm speaking about leadership, I might talk about how that experience has made me more resilient and why adversity is key to making us better leaders. If I'm speaking to a company about their culture, I'll talk about how the experience made me realise what it's like to work in a toxic environment, where psychological safety is non-existent, and the cost of stifling the potential of your team by trying to force them into a mould instead of recognising what they can bring to the table.

Thinking ahead about what message or lesson you need to land will also help you pick the right story and allow you to shape the right conclusion or key takeaway you wish to put across.

My hope is that you keep developing your story bank so that you have a large stock of stories to pick from to land any message you want to put across.

# Audience of One

One of the biggest struggles that often plagues aspiring impact-driven leaders is how to find an authentic voice. The honest truth is that when you talk to your friends or when you catch up with someone you really care about, who you haven't seen in a long while, you're probably not asking yourself if you're using your authentic voice because you're just too busy being yourself, being present, and you're just focusing on the person in front of you. Right? That's your authentic voice!

So why can't we be or do the same in any other setting? What tends to throw people off is the idea of having to address a crowd versus talking to someone on a one-to-one basis. And I get it. Most of us are able to be fully present, to be ourselves, and to share what we have to say when we are in an intimate setting with someone we know and trust, but as soon as we're in front of a crowd it can feel all sorts of daunting and scary.

Now I've heard some crazy things over the years to help people 'get over their nerves', such as, 'Just imagine your audience naked when you talk to them, it will be less scary' or, 'Don't look at anyone in the eyes in the front row, just stare at the back, and keep moving. You'll see, the nerves will ease.'

Now if that works for you, great. But if you're like me, those aren't super helpful.

What works best for me is a technique used by many other authors and creative freelancers: whether you're writing or speaking, focus on just one person.

As counterintuitive as it may sound, the way to get many people to feel what you're trying to convey is to talk to just one person.

Audience of One is the simple exercise of thinking of one person, and one person only, who you would like to reach with your words.

Imagine you're about to speak to an audience. You're feeling all the feels and you'd like to have an easy hack to get over your nerves. Beyond controlling your breath to help centre yourself, there is a magical tool, and that is to put at the forefront of your mind one person who you are trying to reach. This can be someone who is real or it can be someone that you imagine, it can also be someone you know personally and care about that is representative of your ideal audience.

For example, when I know I'm going to be asked to share my story, I will imagine someone I know (i.e. an ideal client) or someone who represents a younger version of myself. This enables me to be clear about who I'm addressing. It removes the abstract concept of an avatar, or what marketers call an ideal customer or your target audience.

If you could reach someone with your story, who would it be? Who comes to mind? Who would get the most value out of hearing your story?

Someone with whom you get excited to share your knowledge and expertise. Someone you want to be able to help. Connect to that one person. Because you will feel a sense of comfort and courage when you do.

That's why every time I've ever stepped on stage or behind a microphone I've always imagined one person in the audience who needed to hear what I had to say. And all I did was focus on that one person.

**If you try to appeal to everyone you end up connecting with no one.**

Keeping an audience of one at the forefront of your mind should make it a lot easier for you to share your story, at least when you're in the writing stage or the workshopping phase of your process.

To this day, I still write every newsletter with 'Dear Julie' in mind, and as I write my emails I imagine that I'm having a breakfast catch-up with my best friend Julie, who also happens to be my life partner and the mother of my kids, and this enables me to feel a sense of safety and honesty that I otherwise wouldn't have if I just thought of someone at random, or imagined I had to address a large audience.

Connecting to one person allows me to touch so many other people. That's why I get so many responses to my newsletters telling me that my readers feel as though I'm in their heads.

From now on, as you continue to go through your journey to impact the world with your story, I want you to bring this person forward. Look at their name. If you have a photo then I want you to have it in front of you when you're preparing what you're going to say.

As I write this book, I have a photo of one of my previous founder and CEO clients who had a tremendous impact on me. Her courage and her story were so moving and the transformation she went through was so great that I know if she had this book in her hands before we met she would have been able to own and share her story a lot sooner.

Donna is my audience of one.

Who is yours?

Let me know by sharing your audience of one on social media using the hashtag #GlowInTheDarkBook. I can't wait.

# Get Started

Once you understand context, platform, audience and message, and have adopted your *audience of one*, it's time to get started on your journey to share your story with the world.

It will be a remarkable experience. Going from holding it all in and running away from it to sharing it with others can be a tremendous relief. A client once said to me: 'Remembering all of it and talking to people about it has just been this huge weight off my shoulders.' Another said: 'I feel like I had been holding on to this secret for so long that I didn't even realise I was holding on any more.'

This is the beginning of your journey, and the start of every journey is the first step.

# Find the Low-hanging Fruit

Make sure you get your laps in.

Stand-up comedians practise their material hundreds of times before they record a special and start getting invited on bigger platforms. You want to make sure you feel comfortable sharing your story and that you've ironed out all the speed bumps that come with sharing a story for the first time.

Even if you spend hours crafting and shaping your story, you won't know how well it lands until you start putting it out there.

You can't learn how to play the guitar by reading about it, you have to eventually pick it up and start strumming the chords. No matter how great or terrible it feels at first, anyone can eventually become amazing if they put in the work.

My suggestion is to start small and work your way up as you become more comfortable. Test things out, stretch a little and see how it feels.

Remember to respect your own boundaries and the boundaries of others. Sharing your stories without boundaries isn't being real or authentic, it's dumping your shit on others, so if you're about to drop a truth bomb or share something emotionally charged, let your audience know about it. Give them a heads-up.

When I shared a story for the first time about my best friend's babysitter who tried to molest me when I was five, I gave the audience a heads-up at the start of the podcast and just before I started sharing the story.

Even though I was hit with an epic dose of vulnerability hangover (the feeling you get after you open up about something that you've been afraid of and feel like maybe it was the worst idea in the world), it eventually felt like a relief and I was glad I'd shared it.

When we share stories, the vulnerability hangover can often convince us we made the wrong choice. It's normal to wrestle with the question of how to know when we've gone too far versus when we're simply afraid. This kind of uncertainty keeps a lot of people from beginning to practise sharing their stories in the first place. And yet, what I've learned to be true is that it is *always* scary to step outside of your comfort zone. These are perfectly normal feelings.

As we saw earlier in this book, our physiological responses to fear and excitement are the same. It's just a question of reframing the experience. There are, of course, moments where you will look back and realise that maybe a different story would have been more appropriate, or the person or platform you shared it with may not have been the right one. But the only way to find that out is to test the waters and build your courage as you go along. Remember, as you start your journey of sharing your story, be patient and compassionate with yourself.

The point is, you need to get out there and start sharing.

It's okay to feel nervous about getting it wrong. The best place to start is to try it out when the stakes aren't too high, where you feel as though you can easily edit, fix or take it down should it not work out.

I remember stepping forward on the bridge across Victoria Falls 110 metres above the ground with a bungee clamped to my feet, thinking, surely this is insanity? My whole body told me to retreat, to lie down on the floor and grab whatever I could. But I knew that if I was to get over my fear of heights, I needed to do it – I needed to override my operating system to get over myself.

And I did, and when I jumped I felt like I'd never felt before. It was total madness, I hated it and loved it! But more importantly, I was so glad I had found the courage to leap beyond my fears.

Sharing your story is just like bungee jumping over Victoria Falls: it's scary as hell, but once you've done it you'll count it among the greatest experiences of your life.

## Exercise

Think of a platform you would like to share your story on, think of the audience on that platform, and determine which story may best serve your intention by picking it from your story bank and customising it based on the formula I shared with you above (context, platform, audience, message).

Go ahead and share that story whether it feels comfortable and make sure to tag me @MarkLeruste and use the hashtag #GlowInTheDarkBook when you do. I'll be rooting for you.

## Show Me You Care

Sharing your origin story helps people understand who you are and what you're about in a valuable and helpful way. Your potential clients are looking for reassurance not only that you are good at what you do, but that you also care about helping them solve their problems. Sharing your story provides an active service to your clients because it helps them avoid having to sort through endless people and brands in order to find the one that can genuinely help them. Your story makes it easy to connect with you. It sets you apart from the pack.

Think about your origin story as an asset that can be part of your growth strategy, that can help you get in the media, attract new clients or sell more books. It really is a gift that keeps on giving.

Shortly after my TEDx talk went live, I received an email from a stranger from across the pond in the US, asking me if I needed any help. He wanted to find a way to work with me, and was happy to do so for free. I couldn't believe that someone who I'd never met in person was willing to donate some of their time simply because of a video they had seen. And yet, Riley McGhee became one of the best things that ever happened to my business. At first we worked together on the run-up to the hundredth live episode of 'The Unconventionalists' podcast, where Riley helped me promote the event. I quickly noticed how efficient, smart, effective and what a pleasure to work with he was. So I asked him if he wanted to continue working with me, as my paid freelance chief operating officer, to solve all my operational issues. Riley agreed. We worked together for a few years before Riley got a full-time job at a start-up as COO. Riley was an anchor, a sounding board and a great friend who helped me through some tough times. When I asked him years later what made him want to reach out to me he told me it was my TEDx talk and how I was willing to be honest, real and share something deeply personal that he, too, could relate to. To this day I receive messages from strangers thanking me for my talk. I still get asked to be featured in media or get invited on podcasts because of the stories I shared in my TEDx talk.

Remember: when sharing your story, always do so in a way that's outward-focused, with the goal of helping your audience. That's why you should always aim for your story to be relevant, inspirational and shareable.

# Your Impact Is the Response That You Get

When in doubt, remember that the impact you have is the response that you get. Your intention is one thing, the impact your story has on others may be another.

Be open to understanding the difference and see how the feedback you get may be a good indicator of how your story impacts others (or not). You can readjust as you go along if need be, but know that by simply committing to sharing your story and stepping out of your comfort zone you are a million miles away from where you started.

**Remember, we may not need the whole truth, but we still want the real you.**

# Be a Voice Not an Echo

Too many people go to their graves with their songs unsung.

As I wrote this book, I told my friend Emily that the Trojan horse of the project was *healing*. She called me out on it. She told me to stop calling it my Trojan horse and make it the central premise *and* promise of the book.

Deep down, I believe in the transformational healing power that sharing our stories can have on the world, but sharing our stories actually heals us too.

Whether sharing your story from the stage or at a networking dinner with someone you just met, you will find common points of interest and feel less alone. You will feel your world widen and your horizons expand. That's the ripple effect of opening up and sharing more of who you are in a vulnerable, authentic and courageous way. It's the rising tide that lifts all boats. It really is the gift that keeps on giving.

I've seen first hand what owning your story has done to me and my clients, and my wish for you is that no matter where you are on your journey, no matter how apprehensive you are, you share your story. You have the tools, you have the knowledge and you have the stories inside of you, stories that are waiting to bloom into life, stories that need to be heard and that you need to tell. Sharing your story will change lives, including yours.

And – *don't tell anyone* – my secret dream is that this book sparks a revolution where everyone starts owning their story and sharing their story so that they no longer remain prisoners of their own history and can instead focus on building their legacy. I want people to give back and share their gifts with the world. In doing so, they will inspire others to start owning their stories too, to start to experience the transformational journey of coming home to themselves and accept all of who they are.

One of my biggest life regrets is that I didn't get my grandparents to share their incredible life story of surviving the Second World War and didn't learn more about where I came from. What I wouldn't give to be able to have those stories recorded somehow. But I hope that my book will help plant the seed that starts a movement of stories being told and shared.

I can't do this alone, so if you'd like to help, please start sharing your story. Share this book or recommend it to your friends, colleagues and family.

I may never see the day we all come home to who we are and are able to stand on stage and share our true story authentically with others without being ashamed or embarrassed, but I will sure as hell do my best to do what I can to help you feel seen, heard and understood.

And that, my friend, begins with you sharing your story so the world listens.

This is only the beginning. Use what you learned in this book to find and refine your memories, to sort them into useful stories and to synthesise them into an origin story.

Then go out there and put your stories to work. There are podcasts, newspapers, radio shows, seminars, civic organisations, business associations, support groups, magazines, books and any number of other media and opportunities that need what you have to offer. And there are people suffering in despair and hardship, psychological and otherwise, who need to be lifted up by what you've endured, what you've suffered, what you've overcome. There are thousands of people waiting to hear your story, and if you still think you have nothing of value to say, wait until you receive a message from a total stranger whose life was changed by your message. It will happen. And when it does, your life, like that stranger's, will never be the same.

The world needs your story.

*I can't wait to hear it.*

PS: I'd love to hear from you. You can find me on social media @markleruste and you can also email me at Mark@TheUnconventionalists.com. Let me know what was your biggest takeaway or aha moment that you got from reading this book. I really do read every email.

Remember to check your progress and acknowledge your transformation as a result of reading this book by filling out your Growth Assessment over at www.glowinthedarkbook. com/growth. Share your score with us over at Hello@TheUnconventionalists.com

# Acknowledgements

If the acceptance speeches at the Oscars is your least favourite part of the ceremony, feel free to skip this part...

First of all, I'd like to thank my amazing partner Julie who somehow found it in her to put up with all my crazy projects over the years (including writing this book) and yet still find a way to love me unconditionally for who I am. Tank tops and all. Your patience, support, love, warmth, and contagious smile have become my safe harbour through turbulent times and periods of self-doubt. Meeting you back in 2013 was the best thing that ever happened to me and raising our two children together is by far the greatest story I'll ever be part of. Long live the avocado love breakfast.

To my parents Avril Bateman and François Leruste who did their very best to raise two boys and who always made sure we had plenty of stories to share with our friends and loved ones, by giving us the best life possible. I'm eternally grateful for all the gifts you've passed on to me and rest assured that your stories will live on through your grandchildren, Johnny and me.

To my brother Johnny, thanks for all the stories of us growing up and for showing me that it's okay to argue and disagree, and that there's always more than meets the eye, even if it does drive me crazy sometimes...

To Hedgy, for always having my back, even when I least deserve it and for somehow always finding the wisdom and courage to tell me the truth, especially when I don't want to hear it. I appreciate your support, love and friendship more than you know. Thank you.

To my 96-year-young granny Beryl Bateman, thank you for always being willing to answer all my questions about your life and share your incredible stories about growing up in a different era with me over the phone on a weekly basis. As you often remind me, 'it's all part of the rich tapestry of life'.

To my best friend Denis Duvauchelle, for putting up with me, for always being up for an adventure and for still being my friend despite the sound my nose makes when I breathe...

To my sister from another mother Naomi Thellier de Poncheville, thank you for always picking up the phone and for always checking in on me, I look forward to many more adventures ahead of us!

To David Over, who after replying to my newsletters where I mentioned I was thinking of writing a book became my creative sparring partner and trusted companion to birth this book project by helping me draft my book proposal. I have no doubt that without David's help there would be no book deal. Thank you, sir.

To my editor Jason Tiller, who managed despite my best efforts to turn my mountain of gibberish and thoughts into something that flows more like a symphony. Thank you for helping me birth a book that I know will have a long-lasting impact. Onwards!

To Leila Green, for pushing me to keep writing, even when I didn't feel like it. Having someone in your corner believing in you and pushing you helps a ton, so thank you.

To Sophie Devonshire, whose generosity of spirit knows no bounds, who kindly introduced me to her publisher and was always available for any author meltdown-related questions, thank you.

To Emily Gindlesparger, words cannot express my gratitude for all your wealth of wisdom and patience that you've shared with me over the last couple of years, guiding me from a distance on this emotional roller-coaster process to write and publish a book. I feel privileged to call you a friend. Thank you.

To my publisher Jonathan Shipley, for being the first to show genuine excitement at the vision of my book, even when my book was just a vague idea. Your enthusiasm and belief in me and this project will not be forgotten. Thank you for trusting me.

To the whole team behind the scenes at John Murray Learning and Hachette UK who worked hard to make this book a reality, thank you for all your help and continuous support.

To the *real* Avengers, i.e. Graham Allcott, Jodie Cook, David McQueen, Sophie Devonshire and Christina Kisley, thank you for all your encouragements, support and help during the process of writing and launching this book. Proud to be part of such an incredible and talented group of people.

To Chris Guillebeau, Daniel Priestley, David Fugate, Kizzy Thomson, Tucker Max, Lucy Werner, Alison Jones, Hal Clifford and the team at Scribe Media, you all played a role in making this book a reality in one way or another. Thank you!

This book couldn't have been written without all the incredible people I've met over the years who agreed to share their stories with me. Be it my private coaching clients, audience members at my talks or guests on my podcast. Helping you shine a spotlight on your stories has been one of my life's greatest honours and know that you continue to inspire me and countless others around the world. Please do me a favour and continue to share your stories as far and wide as possible.

To the incredible community members of my newsletter who helped shape and edit this book, in particular Riley McGhee, Kay Thomas, Mark Warman, Emily Gindlesparger and Raquel Ferrer, your input, suggestions and unfiltered honesty have shaped this book to be the best book I possibly could write. Thank you so much.

To all my mentors and coaches over the years, in person or from a distance, thank you for shaping my mind and spirit and for pushing me to continue to serve with an open heart.

To you, the incredible reader, who took the time to read this book, you have everything you need to start your journey and be the change and ripple effect we've all been waiting for. Now is your moment, enough with learning, it's time to start doing! The world really does need your story.

Last but not least, this book is dedicated to my children, Sophie and Louis, who remind me each day what life and love is really all about. May your lives be filled with stories worth sharing. I have no doubt they will. I love you more than words can express. Remember, *there's always a way.*

PS: If by misfortune I accidently forgot to list you in my acknowledgements, know that I appreciate you and hold a special place for you in my heart. Thank you.

# Citations and References

1   https://www.charitywater.org/about/financials

2   https://www.youtube.com/watch?v=JyVGsAYZfFw

3   Caitlin McNamara, 'Rape and Sexual Assault: The After-
    math of a Rape', 'Today in Focus' podcast, 25 March 2021,
    https://www.theguardian.com/news/audio/2021/mar/26/
    the-aftermath-of-a-rape

4   Jaruwan Sakulku, 'The Impostor Phenomenon', *Journal
    of Behavioral Science*, 6(1) (2011), 75–97, https://doi.
    org/10.14456/ijbs.2011.6

5   Studies by Gail Matthews, KMPG, Kajabi and Dropbox/
    School of Life found that 70–84 per cent of people experi-
    ence impostor syndrome.

6   Editor's letter, *Men's Health* (Jan./Feb 2022).

7   Erica McMillan, 'This Is Why You Need to Become the
    Face of Your Business', *Entrepreneur*, 2 August 2021,
    Entrepreneur.com

8 'Apple Music Event 2001 – The First Ever iPod Introduction', *YouTube*, 23 October 2001, https://www.youtube.com/watch?v=kNoSVBCJqLs

9 https://sanctus.io/mental-health-in-startups/

10 https://www.theguardian.com/media-network/2016/mar/22/startup-entrepreneurs-mental-health-risk-business-failure

11 https://www.cnet.com/tech/services-and-software/study-92-of-u-s-2-year-olds-have-online-record/

12 https://variety.com/2022/film/global/uk-film-tv-spend-2021-bfi-report-1235172074/

13 https://www.theguardian.com/media-network/media-network-blog/2014/aug/28/science-storytelling-digital-marketing

14 https://blog.ted.com/what-happens-in-the-brain-when-we-hear-stories-uri-hasson-at-ted2016

15 https://significantobjects.com

16 'The Tim Ferriss Show', episode #480, https://tim.blog/2020/11/18/dax-shepard

17 Dax Shepard, 'Jason Bateman', 'Armchair Expert', 27 August 2018, https://armchairexpertpod.com/pods/jason-bateman

18 https://www.huffingtonpost.co.uk/entry/oprah-at-facebook-incredi_n_954694

19 'Get Out of Your Own Way, Feat. Dave Hollis, with Joel Marion – BTI 63', 'Born to Impact', 10 March 2020, https://borntoimpact.libsyn.com/get-out-of-your-own-way-feat-dave-hollis-with-joel-marion-bti-63

20 https://qz.com/work/1914116/scribe-media-ceo-jt-mccormick-is-reclaiming-the-name-jevon/

21 https://www.linkedin.com/embed/feed/update/urn:li:share:6520889163737239552

22 'She Cheated On Me and That's Not All – Dr. Aria | E56', 'The Diary of a CEO', 2020, podcast hosted by Steven Bartlett.

23 'How to live more naturally with Tony Riddle' The Unconventionalists podcast, Episode #40, https://theunconventionalists.com/episode/40

24 https://www.ted.com/talks/nancy_duarte_the_secret_structure_of_great_talks?language=en

25 'I Have a Dream', *Wikipedia*, 23 July 2022, https://en.wikipedia.org/wiki/I_Have_a_Dream

26 https://lewishowes.com/about/

27 'Dax Shepard on the Craft of Podcasting, Favorite Books, and Dancing with Your Demons (#480)', 'The Tim Ferriss Show', 18 November 2020, https://tim.blog/2020/11/18/dax-shepard/

28 'Addiction, Childhood Trauma and Depression with Joe Wicks (The Body Coach) | E60', *YouTube*, 30 December 2020, https://www.youtube.com/watch?v=OZN7xRCAz58

29  'E34: Dr Aria – Mental Health, Marriage and Mindfulness', https://podcasts.apple.com/gb/podcast/e34-dr-aria-mental-health-marriage-and-mindfulness/id1291423644?i= 1000442778170

30  'Will Smith on Owning Your Truth and Unlocking the Power of Manifestation', 'On Purpose with Jay Shetty', podcast, 19 April 2021

31  https://www.ted.com/talks/ron_finley_a_guerrilla_ gardener_in_south_central_la

32  R. Buckminster Fuller, 'Planetary Planning', *The American Scholar* (Winter 1970/71).

33  You can see it at https://www.youtube.com/watch?v= 7cBncvKbL6o&t=6s

34  Get a free digital copy over at www.glowinthedarkbook. com/resources

35  'The Secret to Having a Bigger Impact with Mike Michalowicz (Ep #142)', 'The Unconventionalists', podcast with Mark Leruste, https://theunconventionalists.com/episode/142

# Further Resources

Although I'm a big believer that the best learning comes from doing (not reading), I also understand that like me, you may find yourself wanting to dive deeper on all things story and are constantly looking for more resources to sharpen your storytelling tools.

Here is a small sample of books and podcasts that can help you on your journey to share your personal story with the world.

### Books

*TED Talks: The Official TED Guide to Public Speaking* by Chris Anderson

*Do Story: How to Tell Your Story so the World Listens* by Bobette Buster

*The Hero with a Thousand Faces* by Joseph Campbell

*How to Make Your Company Famous* by Jon Card

*Storyworthy: Engage, Teach, Persuade, and Change Your Life Through the Power of Storytelling* by Matthew Dicks

*The Storyteller's Secret: How TED Speakers and Inspirational Leaders Turn Their Passion into Performance* by Carmine Gallo

*The Storytelling Animal: How Stories Make Us Human* by Jonathan Gottschall

*The Power of Writing It Down: A Simple Habit to Unlock Your Brain and Reimagine Your Life* by Allison Fallon

*Bird by Bird: Instructions on Writing and Life* by Anne Lamott

*I Got There: How I Overcame Racism, Poverty and Abuse to Achieve the American Dream* by JeVon McCormick

*A Million Miles in a Thousand Years: How I Learned to Live a Better Story* by Donald Miller

*Building a StoryBrand: Clarify Your Message So Customers Will Listen* by Donald Miller

*Story for Leaders* by David Pearl

*The Breakthrough Speaker: How to Build a Public Speaking Career* by Smiley Poswolsky

*The War of Art: Break Through the Blocks and Win Your Inner Creative Battles* by Steven Pressfield

*Key Person of Influence: The Five-Step Method to Become One of the Most Highly Valued and Highly Paid People in Your Industry* by Daniel Priestley

*How I Built This: The Unexpected Paths to Success from The World's Most Inspiring Entrepreneurs* by Guy Raz

*Hype Yourself: A No-Nonsense PR Toolkit for Small Businesses* by Lucy Werner

*The Secret Thoughts of Successful Women: Why Capable People Suffer from the Impostor Syndrome and How to Thrive in Spite of It* by Dr Valerie Young

### Podcasts

*Uncomfortable Conversations with a Black Man* with Emmanuel Acho

*The Diary of a CEO* with Steven Bartlett

*SmartLess* with Jason Bateman, Sean Hayes and Will Arnett

*Startup* with Alex Blumberg (season one)

*The Tim Ferriss Show* with Tim Ferriss

*Ctrl Alt Delete* with Emma Gannon

*This American Life* with Ira Glass

*Uncommon Ground* with Van Jones

*The School of Greatness* with Lewis Howes

*Aubrey Marcus Podcast* with Aubrey Marcus

*Terrible, Thanks for Asking* with Nora McInerny

*The Moth* with Dan Kennedy

*How I Built This* with Guy Raz

*The Rich Roll Podcast* with Rich Roll

*Best Speech* with Mike Pacchione

*Armchair Expert* with Dax Shepard and Monica Padman

For more resources and inspiration go to
www.GlowInTheDarkBook.com

# About the Author

## MARK LERUSTE

Author photo © Lisa Bretherick

As the founder and CEO of the Ministry of Purpose, Mark is on a mission to help entrepreneurs and business leaders impact the world with their message.

Mark gives keynote speeches at industry conferences, Fortune 500 companies, and fast-growth scaleups, including Google, YouTube, Samsung, Method & Ecover, Intuit, L'Oreal, Virgin StartUp, State Street and Oxford Saïd Business School.

Thanks to his creative video CV 'A Dream Job Would Be Nice' that went viral in 2012, Mark previously served as Country Manager of the Movember Foundation, where he helped raise €2.8 million for men's health and enrolled 110,000 fundraisers to take part, winning multiple awards along the way.

Since then, his videos have been viewed over 3 million times online and his TEDx talk 'What they don't tell you about entrepreneurship' has become the most watched TEDxCardiff talk to date.

Mark believes everyone has a story to share and his top UK ranked podcast The Unconventionalists won Best Interview Podcast at the Podcasting for Business Awards 2021 and reached 190,000+ downloads on Apple Podcasts across 100 countries.

Over the years Mark has been featured in *The Wall Street Journal, The Guardian, Elle, Metro* and other major publications.

When he's not speaking, Mark is at home enjoying life in south London, UK, with his family where he tries to keep up with his two young children who keep him on his feet.

For more information visit MarkLeruste.com

## Contact

To find out more about hiring Mark as a speaker or for all media enquiries please visit www.MarkLeruste.com/Contact or email Hello@TheUnconventionalists.com

Website: MarkLeruste.com

LinkedIn: LinkedIn.com/in/MarkLeruste

Twitter: @markleruste

Instagram: @markleruste

Facebook: Facebook.com/MarkLeruste